The
Garland Library
of
War and Peace

The
Garland Library
of
War and Peace

Under the General Editorship of
Blanche Wiesen Cook, *John Jay College, C.U.N.Y.*
Sandi E. Cooper, *Richmond College, C.U.N.Y.*
Charles Chatfield, *Wittenberg University*

Towards a Lasting Settlement

by

G. Lowes Dickinson, Charles Roden Buxton
H. Sidebotham, J. A. Hobson, Irene Cooper
Willis, A. Maude Royden, H. N. Brailsford,
Philip Snowden, M. P., and Vernon Lee

edited by

Charles Roden Buxton

with a new introduction
for the Garland Edition by

Blanche Wiesen Cook

Garland Publishing, Inc., New York & London
1971

Library of Congress Cataloging in Publication Data

Buxton, Charles Roden, 1875-1942, ed.
    Towards a lasting settlement.

    (The Garland library of war and peace)
    Reprint of the 1915 ed.
    1. Peace--Addresses, essays, lectures. 2. Euro-
pean war, 1914-1918--Peace--Addresses, essays, lectures.
I. Dickinson, Goldsworthy Lowes, 1862-1932.
II. Title. III. Series.
JX1952.B85 1972   327'.172   78-147578
ISBN 0-8240-0343-8

Printed in the United States of America

Introduction

World War I radicalized many British reformers. Convinced that the War was the result of power politics which worked against the vast majority of people and for the interests of a select class of businessmen and industrialists, many of England's leading social critics abandoned the Liberal Party and reform politics for the Labour Party and the politics of active dissent. In order to achieve their goals they organized the Union of Democratic Control.

Members of Britain's Union of Democratic Control had close associates in the American Union Against Militarism. Indeed the two organizations were parallel in goals and membership. The people who founded the wartime peace movement in the United States were largely inspired by the efforts of their British counterparts — as they had been several decades earlier when many of the same people founded the social settlement movement. Jane Addams, Lillian Wald, Norman Thomas, John Haynes Holmes, Crystal Eastman, and Roger Baldwin were all influenced by the writings and activities of England's anti-imperialist internationalists: Charles Roden Buxton, Henry Noel Brailsford, Philip Snowden, Irene Cooper Willis, Norman Angell and Vernon Lee. Prominent before 1914 as outspoken suffragists, social reformers

5

and publicists, they had devoted their lives to programs for economic freedom and social justice. They believed that the war threatened democracy and individual liberty and would destroy all the programs for social and economic progress they had worked to institute.

Since Britain's antimilitarists believed that it would be futile to oppose war once it had been declared, they lobbied against the undemocratic excesses which they believed always accompanied war, opposed secret diplomacy, campaigned for free speech and press in wartime, and emphasized the need for democratic control of foreign policy. Their overriding concern was expressed in a program to insure permanent peace. Towards A Lasting Settlement *was a collaborative work by several of the most notable members of the Union of Democratic Control. They hoped that their essays would provide the guidelines upon which such a peace might be founded.*

G. Lowes Dickinson, *fellow of King's College Cambridge from 1877 and noted author and pacifist, wrote that the basis of permanent peace was disarmament. Dickinson also explored the whole issue of patriotism and asked whether men went to war because they were patriotic or because national chauvinism was inflamed by official propaganda for war. He concluded that "Every war is a war of defense in the eyes of the nation waging it." No nation could any longer stand the public opposition to a war which might appear unnecessary or*

6

avoidable. England, for example, insisted that the European War was to oppose "German aggression and not for English domination"; although the nation would willingly acquire territory once in the war.

Charles Roden Buxton, the editor of Towards A Lasting Settlement *and a noted Labour Party pacifist, believed that democracy had not yet been achieved because its progress was "constantly interrupted by war." Buxton insisted that nationality, or the right of a state to assert its nationalism, was merely one "form of the democratic principle." He pointed out that in all previous peace treaties "the claims of nationality have been flouted," resulting in renewed wars. Buxton concluded, therefore, that the establishment of democratic internationalism was the major foundation upon which to build a lasting peace.*

For J. A. Hobson there would never be durable peace until the economic causes of disharmony were removed. Hobson, a Labour economist who anticipated much of Keynesian economic theory, had attacked British imperialism as early as 1902. He wrote that British imperialism was motivated by the interests of "certain classes" which work against the interests of the entire nation. If nations internationalized their economic interests the probability of continual war would be, Hobson believed, significantly reduced.

A. Maude Royden, a leading suffragist and committed pacifist who opposed both World Wars, pointed out in her essay, "War and the Woman's

7

Movement" that there was no essential difference between the attitudes of men and women toward war. In fact, she wrote, women who have been ostracized from the physical excitement of war have been eager to indulge in its vicarious glories by mourning the death and suffering war created. But, Royden asserted, the "Woman's Movement is one of the great influences making for peace," because militarism is "the real enemy of women" who in wartime have no valued place. What Royden failed to foresee was that women during wartime would be integrated into the economic life of Britain as had never been possible in peacetime.

H. N. Brailsford, a Labour Party journalist and war correspondent, was among the first British anti-militarists to promote the idea of an organization for permanent peace. Brailsford's projected organization was very similar to the one for which America's League to Enforce Peace lobbied. It was an organization in which nations would act in concert and use a collective military force to prevent international war. He also wanted individual nations to retain the right to go to war if arbitration failed. However moderate his own vision of an organization for world peace, he condemned the League of Nations which ostracized the defeated powers as "the expression of the mind of the capitalist classes in Great Britain and France" and claimed in After the Peace *that the League revealed the competitive and imperial motives behind the Treaty of Versailles.*

INTRODUCTION

The last two essays in Towards A Lasting Settlement *are devoted to the concern which first brought the essayists together: their commitment to the extension of democracy and belief that the democratic control of foreign policy would enable states to substitute law for war. Philip Snowden, chairman of the Independent Labour Party and Vernon Lee, a distinguished author and suffragist, agreed that secret diplomacy made war possible because the people were kept ignorant of its causes and were, therefore, the victims of selfish interests which sought, as Vernon Lee wrote, to "establish security by violence and to vindicate liberty by brute compulsion."*

The essays in this anthology raise most of the questions which have been raised again by the war in Indochina: the relationship between honor, patriotism, and war; the use of secret diplomacy and governmental duplicity in the course of war as well as to block arbitration and the establishment of a humane peace; and the damage to democracy caused by the responses demanded by militarist states from their citizens. The essayists believed that the way to insure peace was through the establishment of a truly international organization which promoted free trade, political amity and the democratic control of foreign policy by enlightened self-governments. Several wars later their vision has yet to be seriously tried.

Blanche Wiesen Cook
Department of History
John Jay College, C.U.N.Y.

TOWARDS A LAST-ING SETTLEMENT

GEORGE·ALLEN·
·&·UNWIN·
PUBLISHER·LONDON·
·LIMITED·
·RUSKIN·HOUSE·

TOWARDS A LASTING SETTLEMENT

BY

G. LOWES DICKINSON, CHARLES RODEN BUXTON,
H. SIDEBOTHAM, J. A. HOBSON, IRENE COOPER
WILLIS, A. MAUDE ROYDEN, H. N. BRAILSFORD,
PHILIP SNOWDEN, M.P., AND VERNON LEE

EDITED BY

CHARLES RODEN BUXTON

L'avenir est à qui le fait

LONDON: GEORGE ALLEN & UNWIN LTD.
RUSKIN HOUSE   40 MUSEUM STREET, W.C.

First published in 1915

PREFACE

THE writers of this book are united in one predominant aim : that of securing that a world-catastrophe such as the present shall never recur. We discuss neither the responsibility for the war nor the conduct of it. Our main concern is with the broad problems which will inevitably arise for discussion both at the settlement of the war and for long afterwards. These are the problems of nationality and territorial rearrangement, of the revision of maritime law, of economic opportunities in the colonial world, and, above all, of a real guarantee against war, based on general international co-operation.

While offering no final solution, we believe that there exists, however little it may as yet be defined, a common European policy which would be acceptable to reasonable men in all countries, if only the present atmosphere of panic and prejudice could be dissipated. Already the outline of such a policy is discernible behind the thick veil of half a dozen censorships, each striving to suppress every sign of reason and moderation among the people it controls. Our book will help, we believe, to make the outline clearer.

We deal, further, with the reasons why the new international system, if it is to provide security for the peace and progress of the world, must be founded upon the consent, not merely of the governments but of the peoples. We touch upon some deeper questions which it is impossible to ignore in considering the foundations of permanent peace—the relation of war, for example, to self-government and to the interests of womanhood.

We do not profess to treat all these vast problems exhaustively. Our aim is rather to set people thinking upon them, and so to assist in building up a public opinion capable of appreciating and solving them.

It is natural that there should be many divergences of opinion among the writers of a book covering so wide a range of subjects. We have made no attempt to impress upon our book an artificial uniformity. Each contributor is responsible only for the opinions which he or she expresses.

C. R. B.

CONTENTS

THE
BASIS OF
PERMANENT
PEACE

THE BASIS OF PERMANENT PEACE

By G. LOWES DICKINSON

WHEN the war burst upon the world, the effect upon ordinary people who had not followed the course of foreign affairs was, first, a shock of incredulity, then a feeling "Never again ! This must be the war to end war." As the war has proceeded this feeling has become submerged. The men are fighting, the women are nursing, all are preoccupied with the actual events of the campaigns, the hope of victory or the fear of defeat. In the course of the waging of the war the purpose of it is in danger of being forgotten. But that purpose, nevertheless, lies deep in the hearts of the peoples and animates some, at least, and the best, of their rulers. The nations are fighting to secure a durable peace. Those at the front have not the opportunity to consider the conditions of such a peace. All the more, then, is it the business of those at home to do so. If they neglect it, they are betraying the men who are risking and giving their lives.

Now, though much has been written and said about the war and the peace, very little of it is helpful to this main purpose. In all nations the object has been to throw the blame for the war upon the enemy, and to conclude that all that is necessary is to defeat or to crush him. On this line of approach there is no hope of securing a durable peace. The causes of war lie deeper than the immediate occasions of this war. And a peace which should merely register the defeat of one or other of the groups of Powers, while leaving unchanged the system, the passions, and the ideas that govern international politics, would be merely, as every previous peace has been, a truce before the next war. I propose, then, in this chapter, to discuss, not the ten days of diplomacy that immediately preceded this war, but the general state of things that makes war continually imminent. For it is that state of things that we must change, if we can, to ensure a durable peace.

For centuries past the States of Europe have been armed against one another, and commonly grouped in hostile alliances. Imputed aggression on the one side, fear and suspicion on the other, have been the motives of international politics ; and they have worked inevitably for war. In such a state of affairs, beliefs and suspicions may be more important than real intentions. For intentions can never be certainly known, since it is the tradition of diplomacy to conceal them ; and though every nation asserts the honesty of its own representatives, none credits that of the representatives of its rivals. The fear of war may thus produce war, even though there be no other cause. That is the first point upon which I wish to dwell.

I will illustrate it from the position in Europe during the ten years preceding this war. During that period the States were grouped in two hostile combinations : the Triple Alliance of Germany, Austria, and Italy on the one hand ; the Triple Entente of England, France, and Russia on the other. Between these groups was the tension of suspicion and fear. Genuine attempts were made from time to time to relax it. They failed, because of the mutual mistrust. That the Powers of the Triple Entente were suspicious of Germany does not need demonstration to Englishmen. But equally the German Powers were suspicious of the Triple Entente. The English reader may be inclined to dispute this. He is of opinion, not only that the Entente had nothing but defence in view, but that the Germans knew and believed this. On this latter point I believe he is mistaken. The Germans, there is every reason to suppose, believed that the Entente was a hostile and aggressive combination directed against them. The fact that they say so will probably not weigh with the English reader. But perhaps he may be willing to listen to the considered opinions of the representatives of the Power that has suffered most cruelly at the hands of the Germans. There have been published recently [1] a series of dispatches from the Belgian representatives at Berlin, Paris, and London during the years 1907-14. In these dispatches the view I have attributed to the Germans constantly occurs—that the Entente is an aggressive combination directed against Germany and that it is breaking up the peace of the world. Thus, for example, Baron Greindl, Belgian representative at Berlin, writes on May 30, 1908 :—

[1] In the *Norddeutsche Allgemeine Zeitung.*

" Call it an Alliance, Entente, or what you will, the grouping of the Powers arranged by the personal intervention of the King of England exists, and if it is not a direct and immediate threat of war against Germany (it would be too much to say that it was that) it constitutes, none the less, a diminution of her security. The necessary pacifist declarations, which no doubt will be repeated at Reval, signify very little, emanating as they do from three Powers which, like Russia and England, have just carried through with success, without any motive except the desire for aggrandizement, and without even a plausible pretext, wars of conquest in Manchuria and the Transvaal, or which, like France, are proceeding at this moment to the conquest of Morocco, in contempt of solemn promises, and without any title except the cession of British rights which never existed. The Triple Alliance has guaranteed for thirty years the peace of the world, because it was directed by Germany, who was satisfied with the political division of Europe. The new grouping menaces the peace, because it is composed of Powers who aspire to a revision of the *status quo*, to such a degree that, to realize this desire, they have silenced secular hatreds."

Baron Greindl, it may be said, had been impregnated with the German view. Very likely. But that view is constantly recurring in the dispatches, not only of his successor at Berlin, but of his colleagues at London and Paris. Now England, now France, now Russia, is represented as the danger to peace ; never Germany. The Belgian ministers, it will be urged, were mistaken. They

may have been.   But that is not my present point.
I do not cite the dispatches as evidence of fact.   I
cite them as evidence of opinion.   And I argue
that, if the Triple Entente could be, and in fact was,
thus regarded by neutral outsiders, it must *a fortiori*
have been so regarded by Germans.   We may take
it, then, to be established that the grouping of
the Powers produced, on both sides, a state of
suspicion and fear.   Whether on one side or on
the other, or it may be on both, there were, at
one time or another, actual aggressive intentions,
I do not here discuss.   I do not believe that we
definitely know, though of course we may conjec-
ture and infer.[1]   But even though there never had
been such intentions on either side, the belief in
them was enough to produce a situation pregnant
with war.   The war may have been a war of
nothing but mutual fear.   And this possibility is
not ruled out because, at the last moment, it was
Germany that made war inevitable.   For it may
have been, and, as I believe, was, precisely the
conviction of Germany that war was in any case
inevitable that finally determined her to plunge into
it.   I offer no excuse for her action.   But I think it
has been too much dwelt upon, to the exclusion of
all that lies behind it.   When there is such tension
as we have described in the European situation,
some Power or other will always be tempted to
precipitate the catastrophe, and some Power or
other will always succumb to the temptation.   I

[1] To avoid unnecessary misconception I will say that it is
not my belief that British policy has been aggressive during
the period under consideration.

ask the reader most earnestly to consider whether this is not true ; and for the purpose, to concentrate his mind, not upon the ten days of negotiation, but upon the whole situation out of which that confused and agonized correspondence proceeded. So only can he get a true perspective from which to view the possibilities of future peace.

And observe, further, the situation made a mutual understanding, I will not say impossible, but very difficult. For there can be no understanding where there is no confidence. And it is precisely confidence that is lacking among the representatives of the States of Europe. They always believe, one might say it is their duty to believe, that the others are trying to overreach them. Let me illustrate this from the efforts made in 1912 towards a *rapprochement* between Germany and England. We have now two accounts of these negotiations, the German and the English ; and though these accounts do not altogether agree, the main facts are plain. The Chancellor (this is the German account), believing that Germany was threatened by aggression from France and Russia, was anxious to secure the neutrality of England in case of such an attack. He proposed, therefore, that England should pledge herself first to absolute neutrality ; then, when this was rejected, to neutrality if war were " forced upon " Germany. Sir Edward Grey did, in fact, intend to remain neutral in such a contingency. But, as he stated, he objected to the pledge required ; first, on the ground that it would be misunderstood by France and Russia ; but secondly, because of the impossibility of determining, if war should break out, who was the aggressor. Germany might push Austria into war with Russia, then come in herself, under her agreement with her ally, and yet maintain that the war had been " forced upon " her, and that England was bound to neutrality. On these grounds Sir Edward rejected the German proposal. But he made a counter one. He was ready to pledge England " neither to make nor to join in any unprovoked attack " upon Germany. But now it was the Chancellor's turn to be suspicious. How was it to be known whether an attack were " provoked " or " unprovoked "? Russia, let us suppose, makes war upon Austria, but in such a way that Austria can be plausibly represented as the aggressor. Germany and France are drawn in. And what is the worth of the British guarantee? England will say that the German Powers were the aggressors, and side with her allies. Some such thoughts, we may be sure, passed through the mind of the Chancellor. German suspicions were the counterpart of British, and appeared to Germans as much justified by the situation. And once more, the point is, not whether either Power, or which, was plotting duplicity. The point is, that duplicity was bound to be suspected on both sides. If the relations between the States of Europe were open, honest, and frank, such situations could not occur. As things are, they must occur, and they will continue to occur so long as Europe continues to be organized as it is. The nations are bled to death because they or their statesmen cannot

2

trust one another.   There is the bottom fact.   And it is more important to recognize this fact than to spend our time in looking for the criminal nation.   Such inquiries can seldom be impartial, and they divert our attention from the main point. Wars proceed from the armed peace.   No one may want war, and yet war may come.   So long as there is a system of States, armed one against the other, so long as the relations of these States are governed by suspicion and fear, so long as there is no machinery, recognized and generally used, for dealing with disputes otherwise than by war, so long will war break out, even though neither statesmen nor people desire or choose it.

My first point, then, is that the system of armed States which I have described is enough of itself to produce war, even though there were no other cause than their mutual fear and suspicion. And if this be true, if there be only some measure of truth in it, then one of the conditions of a durable peace is the reorganization of Europe on a new principle.   How that reorganization might be achieved is discussed in a later chapter, and to that I refer the reader.

But it will, of course, be alleged, and with truth, that there are other and deeper causes of war.   Let us, then, consider some of these.

It is often said of wars, and it is sometimes true, that they are wars for freedom against op-pression.   What does this mean?   It means that one of those groups which we call nations desires to conduct its own affairs without

interference, and that some other group desires
to coerce it.   This fact of belonging to such a
group, with the counter fact of not belonging, and
not wishing to belong, to another such group, is a
bottom fact of the contemporary world.   Let us
try to understand its character and limitations.

In time of peace, in most countries, the consciousness of the nation, or State, is latent.   Germans, it is true, have been carefully trained to
regard all their activities from the point of view
of the State.   They are told to study for the State,
to invent for the State, to manufacture for the
State, to trade for the State.   Whether really
they do so or no I do not presume to judge.
But elsewhere, the life of men passes without
much direct reference to the State.   Whatever objects men pursue, be they low or
high, they pursue for the sake of those
objects.   If they are merchants or manufacturers,
they want to maintain and develop their business.
If they are men of science, they want to discover
and to apply their discoveries.   If they are artists,
they want to create.   If they are teachers, they
want to teach.   If they are preachers, they want
to improve morals and religion.   If they are phil-
anthropists or social reformers, they want to make
life better, juster, and happier.   In all these
activities, patriotism is seldom a direct motive, nor
are they at all necessarily confined to the people of
one's own State.   Trade, by its nature, is cosmopolitan, whatever barriers States may throw
across its paths.   So is science.   So, above all,
is religion, if it be true religion.   No Christian, at

least, in time of peace, would maintain that God is the God of the Englishman or the German but not of any other nationality. Thus, in the normal course of life, the idea of the State is not, for the ordinary man, a motive of action. But let his State be threatened, or seem to be threatened, by another ; let it be, as he thinks, insulted ; let any kind of aggression be suggested upon its independence or its honour, and suddenly there flames up in him a passion which, perhaps, he never before knew was there. This passion is the basis of patriotism. According to the whole character, training, and experience of a man, it may assume any form, high or low. It may find vent in the basest jingoism, or in the noblest devotion. Good or evil, or mingled of both, it is a tremendous, fact. And it is one of the facts that lie behind and make possible war in the modern world.

But does it produce war? Do men go to war because they are patriotic? Or does patriotism flame up because they are threatened by war? To judge by the declarations of men, the former never occurs, the latter always. Every war is a war of defence in the eyes of the nation waging it. It may not be so in the eyes of statesmen. Statesmen may utilize patriotism to carry out aggression ; so, at least, every nation is ready, to believe of the statesmen of other nations, and even, on occasion, of its own. But few are ready to admit that patriotism of itself would prompt a war of aggression or conquest. We must, however, probe more deeply behind what we say or consciously think, to what our passions really urge. The lowest form of patriotism, and its commonest form, is but a larger egotism. Men who are insignificant as individuals acquire a sense of extended life by belonging to a powerful nation. They feel a pride in thinking of the number of the population of their nation, the number of square miles of their Empire, the number of " black " men they vicariously govern. They do enjoy, in that gross way, the sense of power. And though they might not avow their support of a war aimed at domination, they will secretly or openly enjoy the fruits of it. If the reader is inclined to question this, I would ask him to consider what his real feelings were when he heard of the conquest of South-West Africa, and what he believes to have been the feelings of most of his fellow-countrymen. The English insist in this war, and genuinely believe, that they are fighting *against* German, not *for* English domination. But how do they feel when, as a matter of fact, they acquire territory? They did not go to war for it. No ! But they are very glad to have it !

There is, then, a side of patriotism, as it is felt by modern nations, which supports, if it does not prompt, wars of aggression. But such wars are the necessary presupposition of wars of freedom. Both kinds of war spring from the same root, the feeling of belonging to a group. As a feeling *for* our own group it prompts wars of defence. As a feeling *against* other groups it winks at wars of aggression. Yet, in either case, though it be a condition, it is not the maker

of wars.   For it does not act unless it is evoked.
And what evokes it are particular situations,
the handling of them by diplomacy, and the
appeals made by statesmen, journalists, and
publicists.   There is, indeed, one region in
modern Europe where a long course of oppression has driven the whole mass of the people
into wars they themselves originate and wage.
But the conditions of the Balkan peninsula are
altogether exceptional.   And though it was trouble
there that unchained the present war, the war was
not, in its origin, for the other States concerned,
a war of peoples.   It was a war of diplomatists,
soldiers, journalists.   But behind these there rallied,
at the outbreak of the war, the passion of patriotism.
We must, then, admit that passion to be a condition of war ; but we cannot admit it to be a
necessary cause.   For, we may urge, let the peoples
be enlightened, let them be led instead of misled,
let them be taught the causes and the consequences of wars, and they would never consent
to make wars of aggression, and therefore would
not need to wage wars of defence.   The instruction
of public opinion and, as a consequence of that
instruction, its growing control over international
politics, would seem to be the remedy here.   And
that point, too, it is the object of this book to
discuss and urge.

But it is not only in tolerating wars of aggression
that the baser forms of patriotism threaten the
peace.   It is in the refusal to entertain the
idea of give and take, of reasonable arrangements, and peaceable settlements between nations.

To the Jingo the bare idea of a concession to another nation is apt to present itself immediately as a humiliation.   Between himself and the individual members of another State he can recognize all sorts of relations, moral, intellectual, and spiritual.   But between his nation, acting as a whole, and that other he recognizes no relation but that of force.

A recent illustration will make this plain.   Some months ago the head-master of Eton, discussing international relations, observed that, if these are ever to be improved, it must be by the road of mutual concessions.   Taking as an example a point that is sometimes mooted, the internationalization of certain waterways, he argued that if we desired that régime to be extended elsewhere, say to the Kiel Canal, we must be prepared to extend it, say, to the Straits of Gibraltar.   The advisability or the practicability of such a policy is no more part of my present argument than it was, if I understood him rightly, of Dr. Lyttelton's.   But observe the effect !   From all the press there went up a universal cry :   " What !   Give up something ! *We* give up something !   WE ! "   Journals once pacifist rivalled their Jingo contemporaries in astonishment, indignation, and contempt.   And *The Times*, dismissing the head-master with a valedictory article of reproof and forgiveness, warned him that, though it may be appropriate for the head of a great public school to talk " in the abstract " of peace, comity, and justice, he must never venture to apply any of these conceptions to the concrete facts of the British Empire.   Now, this spirit is simply a manifestation of corporate egotism. It is the brute, unreasoning reaction of one Being against another, and has no moral quality at all, still less a good one. It is mere instinctive feeling, as independent even of intelligent calculation of self-interest as it is of any higher sentiments. And so long as that feeling is the main motive of those who instruct us in politics, and while these can count upon an instant and unreflective response in public opinion, there can be little hope of any change for the better in the relations of States. It is not enough, even if it be true, that we have abandoned wars for domination. We have to go farther. We have to enter with other States into permanent agreements for the purpose of guaranteeing peace. And, to do so, we have to make, not merely to take, concessions. The point in which this will come home to us is the point of the "freedom of the seas." I do not here attempt to elucidate that ambiguous phrase, nor to discuss the difficult and vital questions which it covers up. But I do urge upon the reader that the question is one for discussion and negotiation, not for indignant and peremptory reprobation. And, in saying this, I have behind me the authority of Sir Edward Grey. In his letter published in the press on August 26th, while rejecting, as of course, a certain German view of what would constitute the "freedom of the seas," he adds :—

" Freedom of the seas may be a very reasonable subject for discussion, definition, and agreement between nations after this war ; but not by itself alone, not while there is no freedom and no security against war and German methods of war on land. If there are to be guarantees against future war, let them be equal, comprehensive, and effective guarantees, that bind Germany as well as other nations, including ourselves."

These remarks of Sir Edward Grey are of the utmost importance. They show, what is evident from other sources, to any one who knows and reflects, that the question of the " freedom of the seas " will be a vital one at the peace settlement. What is going to be the British attitude? Is it to be corporate egotism, self-sufficiency, and pride? Or is it to be a reasoned consideration at once of our own vital interests, and of the equally vital needs of that society of the nations in which we, too, are included?

I have taken a concrete example to bring home my point. But the example must not be allowed to divert the reader from the point itself. What I am urging is that the possibility of war depends at bottom on the existence in individual men and women of the habit of conceiving and feeling their State as independent of legal, moral, and cultural obligations to other States ; of resenting, therefore, all attempts to develop suoh obligations ; and thus regarding it as natural, inevitable, and right that disputes between States should be settled by war. Now, this attitude of ordinary men and women is the greatest obstacle to peace. For every attempt to guarantee peace implies a willingness on the part of the nations to submit their national causes, first, to the rules of a common and recognized morality and law ; secondly, to formal institutions for the application and enforcement of those rules. This is true of every conceivable scheme, from the loosest and freest league to a complete system of international government. There need be, and should be, nothing in any such schemes incompatible with the true interests of nationality, nor with the genuine and desirable autonomy of States. Internationalism does not attack the feeling " We belong to ourselves." It attacks only its perversion, " We do not belong to you." And this point goes very deep. The future of civilization after this war will depend upon the decision of the question whether it is their independence or their interdependence that the nations will stress. The former course leads to a series of wars, the latter to peace. The issue is even now joined. In the passion of war there are those who urge, and apparently with conviction, that national excellence and security lie in the completest possible isolation ; in excluding foreigners and foreign trade ; in exaggerating and perpetuating national differences and national antagonisms ; in fostering, as the chief good, national egotism. That way lies the ruin of Western civilization. For everything that makes for civilization is international. The nations of the West are far more alike than they are unlike, and their points of likeness are much more important than their points of unlikeness. Not only materially but spiritually every nation is poorer by breach of contact with any other. The sole point in which the nations are independent is that of government. That they should retain their political autonomy is desirable, so long as they wish to retain it. And to attempt to bring one of them by force under the government of another is a crime, as well as a folly. But for the growing life of nations, what they need is contacts. Nor is it possible to avoid them. The ideal of independence, spiritual, moral, intellectual, or economic, is as impracticable as it is undesirable. But even a partial movement in that direction may do much harm. For it must increase misunderstandings and points of friction, and so lead to further wars. The cause of peace is the cause of internationalism ; the cause of internationalism is the cause of civilization ; and the enemy of all these is " corporate egotism."

I will not further labour this point. My readers may agree or disagree ; I can only state the issue. But some, even of those who agree that internationalism and peace go together, and that both are conditions of civilization, and most of those who disagree, may meet me with another line of argument. Peace, they may say, may be desirable, but it is impossible ; for the issue of peace or war does not depend upon the will and intelligence of man. The course of history is determined by " laws," and these are not under the control of human volition. States are like living organisms. They grow and expand. And since there is not room for them all to expand indefinitely, they necessarily come into antagonism and war. This kind of fatalism is the stock-in-trade of the champion of war. Here is a characteristic example from Germany :—

" So long as England exists as a World Power, she will and must see in a strong Germany her foe to the death. . . . The war between her and us is not confined to such narrow geographical limits as the war between France and Germany. It turns upon the mastery of the seas, and the priceless values bound up with that, and a coexistence of the two States, of which many Utopians dream, is ruled out as definitely as was the coexistence of Rome and Carthage. The antagonism between England and Germany will therefore remain until one of them is finally brought to the ground." [1]

Now, the plea of necessity here advanced is merely a rhetorical form. It is the passion of the writer for the destruction of England and the aggrandizement of Germany that suggests the necessity of a struggle to the death. Men of this type—and they are to be found in all countries —think in terms of world-conflicts, because they have no other interest in life. It is that way that their imagination leads them. And as they are often men of powerful will, of high position, and of fervid eloquence, they are, and will always be, dangerous opponents. Nothing can meet and conquer them but conviction equally strong on the other side. But this elemental passion is buttressed up by theories that are demonstrably false. Professors and journalists and pseudo-scientists cater

[1] Quoted from a Pan-German organ by the *Forum* of July 1915, p. 164.

like jackals for these lions.   And the doctrine of a necessary expansion of States leading necessarily to war becomes transformed from a formula of ambition to a pretended law of history.   To fully expose these fallacies would require more space than is here at my command.   But the chief points may be briefly indicated.

What is meant by the expansion of a State? Presumably, increase either of population, or of territory, or of trade.   Are these things " inevitable "?   And, if they be, do they lead " inevitably " to war?

Let us take, first, population.   In the past, the growth of population has gone on without the control of will, and may in that sense be called " natural " and " inevitable."   It has also led to war ; because, in early stages of society, increase of population necessitates migration in mass, and the attempt to settle where other people are already settled, and to encroach upon their scanty food supply.   But in the modern world all that is changed.   The development and organization of industry has made it possible to feed an increasing population on a limited area.   And, if migration takes place, it does not involve war. It means merely that producers leave one country to add to the productive forces of another.   Nor is that all.   The growth of population is now under human control.   The birth statistics of all civilized countries show it.   Population need not increase, and, in fact, it tends, in the more civilized countries, to be stationary.   Whether this is a good or a bad thing, or under what conditions it is good or bad, I do not here discuss.   It is enough to have reminded the reader that, in the modern world, neither is increase of population an inevitable fact, nor is it, when it occurs, an inevitable cause of war.   That kind of " expansion," therefore, may be dismissed as irrelevant to the argument.

Let us turn now to territory.   The appropriation of territory can, as a rule, only be accomplished by war, and usually involves further wars to hold it.   And this, of course, is peculiarly true of appropriations of territory in Europe.   It may be said, indeed, with substantial truth, that in Europe, for centuries past, a principal cause of war has been the desire to acquire or recover territory.   But in all this there has been nothing " inevitable."   Annexation is an act of policy, amenable to criticism and reason, and for this policy there are various motives.   Leaving out of account the wars that have been waged by nations to recover the control of a territory that has been filched from them, and confining ourselves to aggressive annexation, we may group the motives under the headings of power, defence, and trade.

Of these, the most common has been the love of power, on the part not of peoples but of their rulers.   And that motive still persists among the Jingoes of all nations.   The present war, for instance, is believed by many people to have been caused solely by the ambition of Germany to annex territory.   However that may be, there have been put forward recently by influential circles in Germany demands for the annexation in east and west of an area of 80,000 square miles and a population of sixteen millions of recalcitrant non-Germans. Is there anything "inevitable" about such demands or about the interminable conflicts that must ensue from the attempts to make them good? Clearly not. No "vital interest" of Germany dictates them. On the contrary, Germans themselves are the first to point out the disastrous consequences of such a policy, not only to the peace of the world but to the German Empire. The whole movement for annexation is based on a false conception of national interest. And the same may be said of any scheme to annex to any nation civilized populations that have not themselves expressed the desire for incorporation. Much of our trouble in Europe has its root in such annexations in the past. There is no intelligent and well-informed man who does not know and admit it ; and who does not, further, know and admit that the well-being, not of Europe only but of every nation in Europe, depends upon the grant of a reasonable autonomy to such alien populations as may continue to be included in any State.

Such annexations, nevertheless, it may be urged, are rendered necessary by considerations of defence ; to "round off" a frontier, to acquire strategic points, to secure the command of home waters. Observe the circular nature of such arguments. You postulate the "inevitability" of a future war ; and, in order to secure yourself, you take the very measures that provoke it. Thus the Germans annexed Alsace-Lorraine, largely for strategic reasons, with the result that they had a permanent menace on their western frontier. Thus the Italians, we have reason to suspect, in order to secure the command of the Adriatic, propose to annex a population of recalcitrant Slavs, and thus to precipitate a war which otherwise need never have occurred. On such lines has the human mind worked hitherto in international affairs. Is it not time that the plain man gave some attention to the matter, and began to inquire for himself into the principles and practice of the " experts " on whose judgment he has hitherto been content so passively to rely?

But I shall be told I am omitting the one important consideration. It is not mere lust for conquest that drives modern nations to annex territory, nor is it necessities of defence ; it is the " vital interest " of markets and trade. Germany, for instance (let us take that case), desires to incorporate Belgium and Holland for the sake of outlets for her trade. What ! But already German trade passes freely up the Scheldt and the Rhine ! It is not necessary to " own " a country in order to send trade through it. " No ! But if the country be not your own it may always interfere with your trade ! " It may ! As Austria-Hungary, for example, has done with Servian trade, as Italy, in possession of Trieste, might do with German trade. The fear is legitimate. But on what is it based? On no " natural necessity," but on human policy. These situations arise because nations believe that they can benefit them-

selves by hampering other people's trade, and that
it is right to do so. But they are mistaken in
thinking that they so benefit themselves ; and, if
they were not mistaken, they would still be wrong
so to act ; wrong, in the first place, because it is
mean and base to try to make other people poor
in order that you yourself may be rich ; wrong
because, even if that be not admitted, the policy
in question is an underlying cause of war ; and
no supposed economic advantage could balance the
material and spiritual evils of war. Wherever it
is claimed that economic necessity compels annexation, the answer is, " free trade " or " free
transit." That is the alternative to annexation
and consequent war. Who would not really choose
it, once the issue were fairly and squarely put?

The same argument applies to the competition
of nations for markets and concessions in undeveloped countries. Such competition is one of the
root causes of the friction that leads to war. The
Morocco crisis illustrates the point. Twice Europe
was on the verge of war because France was determined to annex Morocco, and because Germany
feared (not without good reason) that she would
pursue there her traditional policy of excluding all
other nations from the trade and resources of the
country. And the Morocco crisis was one element
in the complex situation out of which the present
war developed. But in that crisis there was
nothing " inevitable." So far as the economic
factor was concerned, it was French policy that
caused the danger, not international competition.
Let the nations in all such cases not only formally

adopt but loyally carry out the principle of the " open door " ; let them determine to co-operate or to compete openly and honourably in all such areas ; and the danger of war from that cause is conjured. Human policy, not natural necessity, governs the whole issue. There may indeed be trade wars in the future, as there have been in the past. But it will not be because of a historical law. It will be because of the ignorance, the stupidity, or the short-sightedness of corporate interests, peoples, or governments.

I have said enough, I hope, to indicate to the reader how baseless is the assumption that the rivalry of nations " inevitably " brings them into war. It will so bring them if it is wrongly handled, if wrong feelings and false ideas continue to prevail in the future as they have prevailed in the past. But there is no fatality in the matter. It will be as the nations choose and will it to be. Behind wars is not a blind necessity, but causes, definite, ascertainable, and removable. I have tried here to indicate some of the principal of these. They and their remedies are discussed more in detail in later chapters. Meantime, let me sum up the contentions of this one. The first and most obvious cause of wars is the armed peace itself ; and I have suggested to the reader that this cause alone would be sufficient. If we could get rid of armaments and of fear, we might get rid of war. The attempt is sometimes made to attack this problem from the side of armaments. But in fact it seems idle to hope that nations will discard armaments until they feel security. For that reason in this book the problem of armaments is not separately and prominently attacked. The attempt rather is made to show how security might be attained. Given that, disarmament would follow.

Security, however, can only be attained by international agreement ; and international agreement requires the international mind. For that reason I have dwelt upon that aspect of nationalism which makes it the enemy of internationalism and that form of patriotism which expresses itself in antagonism to other nations. That there is a truer nationalism and a finer patriotism I not only admit, I maintain and insist. But that kind not only is not opposed to, it demands, international organization. For it demands peace and goodwill ; and these things · cannot otherwise be attained. I ask the reader, therefore, to correct in himself that habit into which we have all fallen of regarding the absolute independence of States as essential to their well-being, and to modify the feeling which is at the root of that habit. So only can he be prepared for those concessions to international comity which are essential if Western civilization is to be preserved. Further, I have urged that just as a true and desirable nationalism is not incompatible with an organized internationalism, so is the reasonable pursuit of national aims and interests not antagonistic to the pursuit of similar aims by other nations. Nations must compete as individuals must ; but they are no more bound there-

fore to make war than individuals are to fight
duels.   The aims of nations, so far as they are
legitimate, are not mutually incompatible.   And
so far as they are illegitimate they ought to be
abandoned.   Political and economic aggression—
that is, the policy of conquest and of " Protection "—is what brings nations into war.   These
policies are mistaken, as much from the point
of view of the welfare of the individual nations
as from that of international comity.   That the
growing democracy now coming into control of
affairs should understand this from the beginning ;
that it should not be misled by false doctrines ; that
it should come with a fresh and free mind to the
consideration of these great issues ; and that it
should develop an international control of diplomacy, based upon national control in each country
—that is the condition of a durable peace.   The
aim is neither chimerical nor utopian.   But it is
opposed by very powerful forces.   Some of these
are traditions and impulses strong in us all ; some
are false opinions and false ideals ; some are the
machinations of interested cliques desiring to perpetuate strife that they may fish in the troubled
waters.   All these make for war.   What makes
for peace?   Not religion, not science, not learning, not education.   All these serve war as much
as they serve peace.   There is one only that works
for peace, that human reason which is also human
charity.   With that white sword alone can we
prevail.   Will the peoples seize and wield it as
it drops from the hands of those who should have
been their leaders?   Upon the answer to that
question depends the fate of the world.

NATIONALITY

NATIONALITY

By CHARLES RODEN BUXTON

I

THE idea of nationality is best examined, not by trying to frame a definition which will fit all the facts, but by looking at the facts themselves. The definition will emerge later. What lies immediately before us is a number of peoples who have an intense desire to express, in some distinct form of government, what they conceive to be their nationality. Some, like the Croats, Bohemians, Poles, and Finns, have had such a government in quite modern times. Others have never had it, or had it only in the shape of some transient Empire in the dim past. Some want full independence ; some would be satisfied with autonomy within a larger unit. Some, like the Italians, Roumanians, and Serbs of Austria-Hungary, desire union with an existing free State. Others desire the creation of a new political entity. With some the common bond is identity of language or religion ; with others, the belief that they spring from the same stock and have shared from time immemorial in the same sufferings and achievements. Two things are common to them all. They are all baulked of their hopes, and they are all prepared to make untold sacrifices to realize them.

The nationality principle is merely another form of the democratic principle. To the thorough-going democrat this should be enough. Here are peoples of which the overwhelming majority desire a certain political object. Let them have it, he will say, provided it does not clash with the desire of some larger section which has a right to be heard in the matter. And in point of fact it does not, as a rule, clash with the desires of any such section, but only with the imperialist and militarist ambitions of the ruling classes of some strong State founded on conquest.

And democracy, rightly understood, should carry us a stage farther. For, whether the claims of nationality are reasonable or not, their satisfaction is one of the prime conditions of peace, and without peace democracy is for ever insecure. If sores are left open which cannot be healed without further war, then European democracy, however brilliant its triumphs, will be founded upon a vol-canic crust which may at any time collapse into the molten lava. The principal reason why democracy has hitherto made so little progress is that its march has been so constantly interrupted by war. In almost every peace treaty of the nine-teenth century the claims of nationality have been flouted, and recurring war has been the result.

But are we to ignore the question whether these claims are or are not reasonable? Are we simply to accept them as a primary fact like the law of gravitation? Not altogether, though to those who have felt by personal contact the intensity of the national sense in peoples deprived of their freedom and unity, and the way in which these great words seem to blind them to almost every other thought, there seems to be nothing absurd in the notion. It is not likely that anything we can do or say will make a Bohemian of Prague or a Bulgarian of Southern Macedonia reconsider the rooted instinct which tells him that his spiritual home is a free Bohemia or a free Bulgaria. Yet democracy itself must be founded upon the solid basis of reason and forethought. If the peoples are to work out their own salvation, and co-operate with each other in working out the salvation of all, they must think. They must take into account, not one great fact but all great facts. They must not be led by mere sympathy to throw themselves whole-heartedly into the support of a claim, however strong, which conflicts with the conditions of the modern world. Does the claim of nationality, pure and unmixed, conflict with these conditions? Will it fit into the new environment, the new world which we hope to create for all the peoples after the war is over? What does it really stand for in human life? What can it give to the world? With what dangers, if any, does it threaten the world?

At this point, at which we come to closer quarters with our problem, we need to ask ourselves a little more exactly what it is. A German newspaper writer remarks that Germany would readily give up Alsace-Lorraine, Posen, and Schleswig if Russia would give up Finland, Poland, Samarcand,

Bokhara, and other places, and England would give up India, Egypt, Cyprus, Malta, and Gibraltar. Viewed in this light, we are tempted to say of nationality what Hazlitt said of the opera, " It is a very fine thing ; the only question is whether it is not too fine." Evidently no Great Power will be prepared to accept so wide a definition of nationality as that of our sarcastic German. One might waste a great deal of time in arguing about the border-line of the subject. Let me say, to simplify matters, that I rule out, for the purposes of the present chapter, the peoples of India, Egypt, and Persia. The nationalist movements of these countries make a strong appeal to our sympathies. There are many Englishmen who are prepared to help them forward. But to place them with those of the European nationalities would be to misrepresent the significance, and belittle the force, of the latter. I am speaking, then, in the main, of certain specific peoples—Alsatians and Lorrainers, Italians, Finns, Poles, Bohemians, Ruthenes, Roumanians, Serbo-Croats, Bulgarians, Greeks, and Armenians. I omit the Irish, on the assumption that some form of national self-expression is now assured to them.

II

It will be as well to recognize at the outset that there are several difficulties in the way of a full application of our principle. Roughly, they may be divided into two classes—those which make the observance of strictly national frontiers inconvenient on economic and strategic grounds, and

those which are inherent weaknesses in the principle
of nationality itself. Let us take these in order.

Nature, migration, and conquest have disposed
the population of the world without any regard
to the best economic units or the most defensible
boundary lines. The most obvious examples of
the economic difficulty are the Poles, Bohemians,
and Hungarians, who do not occupy any point on
the sea-coast, and who do not possess within their
own borders a sufficient variety of raw material.
Tariff walls, again, often run counter to the
national principle. The producers and business
men of Alsace-Lorraine have for years past made
all their arrangements on the basis of the tariffs,
the markets, the railway, the banking and credit
systems, and the business connections of Germany.
The same may be said, in a lesser degree, of the
economic position of Poland in relation to Russia.
Some of these difficulties could only be completely
surmounted by freeing such ports as Fiume, Trieste,
and Danzig, and the navigation of rivers like the
Danube, Vistula, Elbe, Scheldt, and Rhine, from
all restrictions, others by commercial treaties or
free exchange.

With regard to strategic questions, there are
obvious reasons why, in a world dominated by
the fear of war, the desires of a people for a
national government should have to give way to
the exigencies of fleets or armies. Frontiers have
been settled again and again with a view, not to
the desire of the inhabitants but to military or
naval needs. If we are to escape from this
necessity, we must ask ourselves the question, must

the world be always dominated by the fear of war?

These are difficulties which might conceivably be surmounted in time ; but is there not, it may be urged, something in the nature of nationality itself which is fundamentally opposed to the kind of progress we are aiming at? We sympathize with an oppressed nation, but when we have set it on its feet, does it not become in its turn an oppressor, using the arts of its own former tyrants with an ingenuity born of long experience? Does not " nationality militant," to borrow a term from the ecclesiastical world, pass over into something odious and repulsive when it becomes " nationality triumphant "? In nations that have acquired and established their freedom, in France, in Germany, and in Italy, is not the very word " Nationalist " applied, and naturally applied, to the Imperialist parties, which aim at extending the sway of the nation over other nations? Is not the desire of a successful nation to spread its particular type of civilization essentially the same desire as that which inspires a subject race to defend its culture against that of its rulers? Is not the claim to national self-expression invariably followed by the claim to world-power? In a word, is not the intense desire for national independence, with all that it entails, the direct enemy of internationalism, that wider conception which must inspire the next great step in the progress of the world?

I cannot answer these questions in a manner wholly favourable to the cause of nationality. Nor do I wish to strike a balance between the merits and the demerits of that cause, for the factors are very numerous and perhaps in part incommensurable, and to think out the problem for oneself, unaided and unguided by some one else's personal opinion, is perhaps the most useful process from the point of view of building up an enlightened public opinion. I will content myself with pointing out some practical considerations which have a bearing on the problem.

When nationalities are mixed in fairly equal proportions, as are the Hungarians, Germans, Roumanians, and Serbo-Croats of Southern Hungary, it is true that the principle of nationality is an inadequate guide. But such districts are not common, and we are far from having reduced our problem to these narrow limits. The ordinary case is that of a preponderant nationality with an " Ulster " enclosed in it or mixed up with it. This case can be met, partially at least, by distinct and recognized provisions for the linguistic and ecclesiastical rights of the minority in connection with local government bodies, churches, schools, and other institutions. There is always, no doubt, a difficulty in making these provisions effective ; in the long run this can only be done by assuaging inter-racial hatreds and diminishing the danger of war.

Many of the difficulties which attend the realization of nationality would be avoided if autonomy, rather than complete national sovereignty, were the object aimed at. There is undoubtedly something crude and primitive in the latter claim, in spite of the almost axiomatic character with

which long usage has invested it. In point of
fact, the farther West we go, the more we find
that autonomy, or a freedom restricted by the
requirements of some larger political unit, is
proving a sufficient answer to the national claim.
Irish history during the past century provides a
good example of the change from the one idea to
the other. The farther East we go, on the other
hand, the more we have to admit the dangers
and difficulties which spring from the demand for
unfettered sovereignty. Cruder tyrannies have
produced a cruder reaction. We cannot blame the
Balkan peoples for this. It is unreasonable to
expect them to skip over a stage which has
hitherto seemed indispensable in political development. But it is probable that even in the East
nationalist ideas will become increasingly tinged
by the conception of autonomy.

III

And now, having faced the admitted difficulty
of applying our principle without considerable
exceptions and reservations, we may turn to the
positive contribution which nationality makes to
the progress of the world. The matter must be
looked at from the point of view both of each
nation and of civilization as a whole.

To nations in an early stage of development,
particularly those formerly subject to Turkey,
nationality stands for many things that we in the
West have ceased to associate with the term, and
now value under other names. It means the attain-

ment for the first time of culture, of refinement, of education for their children, of the right to worship as they think fit. To most subject peoples the realization of nationality means the realization also of democratic government. The two aims are largely inspired by the same feelings. In 1848 the French and German struggles were mainly directed to the latter, while the Italian and Hungarian were mainly directed to the former, but neither struggle was exclusively democratic or exclusively national.

So inextricably does the aim of nationality become bound up with other aims, that there is a tendency to think that none of' them can be realized until national self-expression has been secured, and to neglect the steps which might be taken, even under present conditions, to realize them. This is especially noticeable in the Balkans. The whole energy of the nation, both in thought and action, is too often turned into the one channel. Nothing else counts. Education, social reform, honesty in public life, economic development—all lag behind, because all are subordinated to the overmastering passion of nationality.

When it becomes a question, not so much of securing self-government and culture but of securing a particular type of these things as opposed to another type, we are dealing with something a little less tangible, the need for which is sometimes disputed by political thinkers. The members of races subject to Austria and Germany, for example, do not as a rule suffer very seriously if they are content to live a quiet life apart from

all public interests, to shut themselves up within
the circle of their family and friends, to follow
their daily business, and not to take any part
whatsoever in " movements," whether political or
otherwise. If they do, then it is a matter of
police spies, perpetual interference, the suppression
of newspapers, the imprisonment of editors and
thinkers and political leaders, the extinguishing
of every manifestation, however slight it may be,
of anything distinctively national—flags, meetings,
exhibitions, processions, pamphlets, songs, and
books. It means the creation, in a word, of an
atmosphere intolerably depressing and irritating to
men with a belief in progress and in human fellow-
ship. Some will say that the question whether
a certain type of thought and of public life and
social habits shall or shall not prevail, whether
the type shall be French or German, Polish or
Russian, is not a point worth fighting about. Few
would say this, however, if they had experienced
what it means to a people to be denied all political
and " cultural " self-expression. To Englishmen
that experience is so remote that they find it
difficult to comprehend. It is for this reason,
coupled perhaps with a certain contempt for
teachers and artists, that we have actually no
equivalent for the word " cultural," without which
the Polish or Bohemian nationalist would hardly
know how to express himself.

Nationality stands, then, in the mind of a people
struggling to be free, not indeed for the whole,
but for a large part, of what we feel to be good
and desirable in human life. It stands for self-

development and self-expression, in so far as these ends require for their realization a wider sphere than that of individual or family life—the sphere of combination and association, above all of government. It stands for the cultivation of those national habits of life and thought which are dearer to us than others because they are in a fuller sense " our own "—just as family customs and family words have a peculiar savour for us, creating as they do a whole atmosphere, and calling up, without any need of explanatory speech, a hundred common memories and familiar ties. This self-expression, this cultivation of things so dearly prized, is the object upon which a nation's hopes are concentrated in the days of its servitude.

Does the experience of liberated nations justify such hopes? Some think not. They point to tyranny in Hungary and corruption in Italy. They say that the dreams of 1848 and 1860 have faded into something tame and grey, sordid and disappointing. Perhaps the disappointment is only the fruit of an exaggerated expectation. In South-Eastern Europe, where liberation has meant a change from disorder to order, and the reclaiming for civilization of a desert, no one could possibly question the reality of the progress made. But even where the change has been less complete and striking, there has been a gain. Life is wider and fuller for a nation in which the people accept the form of the government and co-operate in working it. Such a nation is a higher political organism than an empire, however vast its extent or however overwhelming its power, in which the

4

citizen is denied the free exercise of his political and associative faculties, except in the heated and morbid atmosphere of resentment and intrigue. There is a gain of inward satisfaction, the removal of a sense of wrong. True, a people no sooner gains its freedom than it begins to crave and strive for something further. Whitman has told us that " from any fruition of success shall come forth something to make a greater struggle necessary." But at least a step on the road has been taken, and we in the West, who conceive all life as a road, feel instinctively that that means an advance to something better.

IV

But it is when we take the point of view of civilization as a whole, not that of individual nations, that we appreciate most fully the value of the national spirit. When our grandfathers and great-grandfathers were fired with enthusiasm for Greece and Italy and Hungary, they conceived themselves to be maintaining, not merely the rights of Greeks, Italians, and Hungarians, but some common and fundamental interest of mankind. It is, in fact, to the interest of mankind that there should exist the greatest possible variety of types of thought and action. The world progresses most when it is able to choose between a wide range of different courses. Those which are inherently good will tend to survive. Those which are trivial or useless will be ignored. No one can judge which should be encouraged and which suppressed

—least of all a single imperial Power or a group of such Powers. The best chance is to let all the varieties bloom and flourish, and to trust to the free choice of humanity to take or leave them. This, the essential doctrine of Liberalism, is not a bloodless abstraction as applied to the matter now in hand. What a treasure-house of civilization is revealed to us in the national life of our fellow-peoples, whether those which have won their freedom already, or those whose dreams and hopes derive more brilliant colour and deeper emotional meaning from the very fact that they are still unsatisfied. Just as England contributes her sense for political liberty, France her intellectual honesty and lucidity, Germany her industry and discipline, Italy her æsthetic aptitude, so Finland has her advanced democracy, Poland her music and art, Bohemia religious independence, the Serbs their warm poetic temperament, the Greeks their subtlety and their passion for the past, the Bulgarians their plodding endurance and taciturn energy, the Armenians their passion for education and progress. And each of these characteristics is merely a faint indication of what is distinctive in the people concerned. Peoples are not, in fact, to be distinguished from one another by a single mark, detaching itself from a background of pure similarity. It is the total combination of qualities, of historical events, of natural surroundings, which makes them what they are—conglomerations of various and conflicting personalities and parties, touched nevertheless with some unifying character which makes even their very divisions distinctive.

National culture may some day give place to cosmopolitan culture, but meantime it is a richer and intenser thing. The poetry of a nation, for instance, gains more from the deep roots of national memory and tradition than it loses from the political boundaries which fence it from the air and sun that might come to it across neighbouring gardens. The whole gains by the fuller development of every one of its parts.

V

It will be noted that the question hitherto discussed is that of nationality, rather than that of " small nationalities." The difference in size has far-reaching consequences. A large nation may be content to rely upon its strong arm ; but if we are to have any hope at all of placing the smaller nationalities, in Mr. Asquith's words, " on an unassailable foundation," we must work out some system of international relations which will secure the right of the weaker State against the aggression of the stronger. We must, in other words, substitute law for brigandage and private defence. We must do in the international sphere what the woman's movement demands that we shall do in the national sphere—recognize that inferiority in physical strength shall be no reason for any kind of disability. Just as inter-individual war, or the possibility of it, precludes the equality of women with men, so international war, or the fear of it, precludes the equality of small nations with large. This shows at a glance the absurdity of supposing that war in itself—the victory of one group of armies and fleets over another—can possibly place the rights of the smaller nationalities on an unassailable foundation. It might for the moment protect Belgium, or Serbia, or Poland ; but it would leave these and all other small peoples in the same position as before, so far as security for the future is concerned. War, and the fear of war, inevitably puts a premium upon large centralized States, because large centralized States are the best means of wielding force. If a few small peoples refuse to yield to this general tendency, they do so at their peril. An international agreement to prevent war would place small nations in a position of security, and nothing else would do it. The ideal of the nationalist, "the independent existence and free development " of all the peoples, would thus be attained.

VI

It is now time to turn to the Great War, and to ask what is its relation to the nationality problem. Each side claims that it is fighting for certain oppressed nationalities. How far can these claims be justified? It is as well to look first at the belligerent Powers and see how far they themselves conform to the principle of nationality. We see at once that, from this point of view, Austria-Hungary and Turkey stand on quite a different level from the rest. It is a misuse of language even to describe them by the same term as countries like England or France,

Germany or Russia. I include the last two
Powers because, so far as subject white nationalities are concerned, they are only offenders to the
extent of about one-seventh of their population.
Broadly speaking, they are nations, with a national
soul and character, while the Dual Monarchy and
the Ottoman Empire are not nations at all, but
composite structures formed by the conquest of
many nations. There is a strange topsy-turvey-
dom in our popular conception of the war. We
entered into it, we believe, for the sake of small
nationalities, yet there is actually a strong current
of pro-Austrianism and pro-Turkism among us,
as is shown by the fact that the savageries of
Austria in north-west Serbia and of Turkey in
Armenia are usually thrown into the background by our press. Historically, of course, this
current is caused by the sympathy of one ruling
race for other ruling races, and by the now dis-
carded anti-Russian policy of the Victorian era.
It is none the less dangerous from the point of
view of the interests of nationality.

The nature and composition of the belligerent
Powers, then, suggests that in this matter of
nationality the balance inclines strongly in favour
of the Quadruple Entente. Nor is this the only
sense in which we are " fighting for nationality."
We English may fairly say that we went to war
for it, in the sense that it was the wrongs of
Belgium which produced the popular enthusiasm
for the war. We may fairly add that our ideas
of self-government, as illustrated in recent times
by our South African policy and our Home Rule

movement, are far in advance of those of other
Empires, and that as a people we earnestly desire
that national claims should receive their due weight
in the settlement. And this is not all. The
Quadruple Entente as a whole may be said to
be fighting for nationality in another sense—the
sense, namely, that its victory could be made to
contribute to the liberation of subject peoples in
a far higher degree than the victory of its enemies.
In order to illustrate the point let us take certain
extreme examples. Let us suppose that either the
Entente or the Alliance were in a position to dictate
terms. The examples are artificial, but they help to
clear our minds. Note, first, that there are certain
nationalities whose position would quite probably
be much the same in either case—the Poles, who
would probably gain autonomy, and the Finns, the
Ruthenes, and the Jews, whose national interests
would probably not be affected. There remain
the Bohemians, the Alsatians and Lorrainers, the
Danes of Schleswig, the Italians of Southern
Austria, the Serbo-Croats and Slovenes, the
Roumanians, the Bulgarians, the Greeks, and the
Armenians.

Now, a victory for the Entente would
(assuming that the settlement were inspired by
nationalist conceptions) satisfy the claims of the
majority of these peoples, numbering in round
figures 30,000,000. A victory for Germany,
Austria, and Turkey, on the other hand, would
make it almost impossible to satisfy any of them,
with two exceptions—the Bulgarians of Central
Macedonia and the Roumanians of Bessarabia,

whose liberation would be more than outweighed by the continued subjection of their brethren in Hungary. No one supposes that the choice is in fact between the freedom or subjection of the whole of these 30,000,000. The actual choice lies, of course, between much narrower limits, because no dictatorship is possible on either side. A partial victory would open the way to correspondingly partial results. But the broad black and white outlines do provide a true picture of the issue which was raised upon the tragic stage of Europe when the Austrian armies crossed the Drina in the summer of 1914. One might almost say that this is the greatest issue of the war, if one interprets the word " issue " as meaning a point which could really be settled by the war, and in all human probability could not be settled without it. This is the real sense in which we are, if we choose—but only if we choose—" fighting for nationality."

How far we are likely to choose this course, how far indeed we shall be in a position to choose it, even if we desire to do so, is another question. In the welter of conflicting interests many things that we should have liked to do will be found to be out of our reach. The fact is that to engage in a European war, and at the same time to be punctilious about nationality, is impossible. Such a war may begin as a struggle of nationalism against imperialism, but it cannot remain so. It must inevitably develop into a conflict between rival imperialisms. In Central Macedonia our diplomacy has led us into the position of supporting Serbian

imperialism as against Bulgarian nationalism ;
while in Dalmatia, if the universal belief is true,
we are endeavouring to substitute Italian for
Austro-Hungarian imperialism, as against the
national claims of the Serbo-Croat population. No
good can possibly come of shutting our eyes to
these incidental results of war. They do not alter
the fact that there are a great number of cases
in which we shall still be free from commitments.
There will be many doubtful issues at the settlement in which the influence of this country will
very probably be decisive, and we must make the
best of these opportunities for helping forward the
cause of nationality.

There remains a final point. We are not likely
to make much of these opportunities if we leave
the whole matter in the hands of the diplomatists.
The tradition of the Foreign Offices of Europe
is wholly indifferent to nationality. It moves in
an atmosphere altogether alien to such ideas.
Diplomacy is much more concerned with the tem-
porary interests of governments than with the permanent interests of peoples. Every peace made
by diplomatists—at Vienna, Paris, Frankfurt,
Berlin, Bukharest—has borne testimony to this.
We cannot take for granted that the statesmen of
the Quadruple Entente—among whom those of our
own country will be in the minority—will go out
of their way to help forward the principle of
nationality except upon one condition. That condition is that there shall be a public opinion, definite,
alive, not to be denied, which shall insist that the
principle be applied. Democratic influence in the

settlement of the war offers the only security that the interests of nationality will be seriously considered. By this it is not meant that every English citizen can be expected to pronounce upon the exact frontiers of Poland, the rights to be accorded to the Hungarian minority in Transylvania, or the methods, whether of plébiscite or of impartial inquiry, whereby the wishes of any given population should be ascertained. There will be different degrees of knowledge, some greater and some less. But we ought not to admit the too commonly accepted idea that the sister nations of Europe can never be more than a name to the English democracy—that the aspirations and the main characteristics, for example, of a noble race such as the Bohemians, with a population one-third of that of England, is a mere detail with which Englishmen cannot be expected to concern themselves. That would be to admit too narrow a range for international sympathy. There is more likelihood to-day than ever before that the sympathy of one democracy for another will be able to break through the age-long conventions of diplomatic intercourse. Let us not be tempted to despair by the cynic who cites to us, from the past conduct of all the governments concerned, painful proofs that they have not cared much for nationality, and that some of them have not even paid it the shadowy compliment of lip service. There is no practical use in seizing upon this obvious opening for scepticism. Let us rather take the declarations of statesmen at their face value, recognizing that the declarations themselves create a new condition of things, that they oblige the Powers which have made them to take steps to realize them, and that there are among the statesmen not a few who are anxious to have behind them a popular demand which will enable them to take these steps. It is the duty of the peoples to see to it that the declarations of their governments are not forgotten.

THE
FREEDOM
OF
THE SEAS

THE FREEDOM OF THE SEAS

By H. SIDEBOTHAM

ONE of the promises of victory is that Great Britain will be able to review her whole naval policy in the light of the experience gained in the war. Sir Edward Grey has himself indicated that such a review may be appropriate in the negotiations for peace after victory has been won, and the object of this chapter is to consider certain issues which, though they are usually evaded now, may then be in the forefront of political discussion. It is known that the United States of America are particularly concerned in this discussion, and German diplomacy in America has omitted no opportunity of presenting its view of the issues. Direct defence of German policy in Europe Count Bernstorff has hardly attempted ; his whole object has been to distract American attention from the sins and crimes of German militarism by making a more formidable bogy of British sea power. That Germany, who in her submarine campaign has been guilty of the most atrocious acts of naval tyranny in history, should still have been able to represent herself as the champion of the " freedom of the seas " without being laughed or hissed out of court in the United States is a paradox which needs much explanation. To leave it unexplained, and to persist in ignoring the existence of a very grave problem of policy, is dangerous to the interests of this country, of which the maintenance of relations of cordial friendship with the United States is not by any means the least important.

The ideal of the " freedom of the seas " is too fine to leave in the hands of the Germans. The meaning of the phrase has greatly changed since Grotius more than three hundred years ago wrote his " Mare Liberum," to vindicate the right of the Dutch to trade with the Indies, and to combat the pretensions of the Portuguese to a monopoly of the seas that they had been the first of Europeans to traverse. The sea captains of Elizabeth had combated the similar pretensions of the Spanish. The sea policy of the Stuarts, however, asserted a definite British sovereignty over the Narrow Seas against the Dutch, and in 1618 John Selden wrote his " Mare Clausum," in which he argued against Grotius that there could and should be a national sovereignty of the open seas precisely similar to sovereignty of land. That controversy ended in the triumph of the view of Grotius, and, indeed, if he had not triumphed British maritime supremacy, which necessarily by its ubiquity transcends the ideas of territorial sovereignty, could never have come into being. The seas are now free, economically and politically, in peace time, and the chief survival of Selden's contentions is the doctrine of territoriality within three miles from low-water mark. In securing this freedom of the seas England has taken a leading part, and any attempt to shackle their freedom with the doctrine of territorial sovereignty would find England at the head of a coalition prepared to go any lengths in resistance. But the freedom now in question is the freedom, not in peace but in war. It is a war problem pure and simple, and the conditions that prevail in peace-time have no sort or relevancy. England, for example, which admittedly is the protagonist of its freedom in peace time, is, in the opinion of her critics, its most powerful opponent in war. The " Mare Clausum " of Selden's day has waited nearly three centuries to reappear in British naval practice in the Proclamation closing the North Sea to shipping which was issued as an answer to the indiscriminate sowing of mines by Germany on the high seas.

The outbreak of the war found our Navy in overwhelming material strength and in a high state of technical efficiency. But it also revealed hesitancy and uncertainty in certain departments of controlling policy. No navy was ever readier to fight a fleet action, and (a few accidents apart) it had carefully worked out the problems of defending our shores from invasion and raid and of securing our sea-communications. Its attack, however, against an enemy who persisted in declining a fleet engagement was only an equivocal success. In particular, its blockade of the enemy's coasts and the strangulation of his commerce were for long enough very partial and hesitating. This hesitancy contrasted markedly with our maritime policy in the war with Napoleon. Then we had

5

no doubts whatever ; we asserted the right to confiscate all enemy's property at sea, whatever the flag under which it was being carried.   The doctrine that a neutral flag might protect enemy's property which was then put forward by the Armed Neutrality was indignantly repudiated. " Shall we," asked Pitt in 1801, referring to the doctrines of the Armed Neutrality, " give up our maritime consequence and expose ourselves to scorn, to derision, and contempt?   No man can deplore more than I do the loss of human blood—the calamities and distresses of war ; but will you silently stand by and, acknowledging these monstrous and unheard-of principles of neutrality, insure your enemy against the effects of your hostility !   Four nations have leagued to produce a new code of maritime law which they endeavour arbitrarily to force on Europe ; what is this but the same Jacobin principle which proclaimed the Rights of Man, which produced the French Revolution, which generated the wildest anarchy and spread horror and devastation through that unhappy country?   Whatever shape it assumes, it is a violation of the rights of England, and imperiously calls upon Englishmen to resist it, even to the last shilling and the last drop of blood, rather than tamely submit to degrading consequences or weakly yield the rights of this country to shameful usurpation."   The passage illustrates the law of history that the more violent the assertion of a principle is in the one generation, the more likely is its repudiation in the next.   Fifty years later by the Declaration of Paris we accepted the principle which Pitt was prepared to shed the last drop of English blood to resist. The Declaration was a great weakening of belligerent powers for the sake of neutral right, a sacrifice of the offence to the defence. The effect of that Declaration was that though the belligerent's flag might be chased from the seas, his trade could not be so long as there was a neutral ship in which it could be carried.

That was not all. More than fifty years after the Declaration of Paris the Declaration of London entrenched neutral rights still more strongly. It drew up a " free list " of articles which a belligerent could (so long as there was no blockade) import through his own ports in neutral ships and through neutral ports if his own ports were blockaded. In this list were many articles of use in war, such as cotton. Further, there was a list of articles of conditional contraband, which could not be stopped except on evidence that they were intended for the use of the belligerent Government. If there was evidence that they were so intended, importation through a belligerent port, even under a neutral flag, might be stopped, but not importation through a neutral port. It followed from these two rules, to take concrete examples, that cotton in war-time could be imported in a neutral ship into Hamburg or Bremen just as though there were no war, and that foodstuffs might be imported through a Dutch port even though there was proof that they were intended for the supply of the German army. These were very grave restrictions of belligerent power at sea as we had exercised it in the Napoleonic Wars. And the railway communications of Europe created since those wars have greatly increased the effect of these restrictions. A hundred years ago, when there were no railways and the roads were bad, to blockade the ports of a country was to prohibit it from supplies over sea. Now the closing of German ports meant no more than the diversion of her traffic to neutral ports, which could not be blockaded. In all the changes of the law made throughout the century two principles are seen to be at work : the principle that belligerent power must yield to neutral rights, and the further principle that war is a relation between Governments, and must not be allowed to interfere with the peaceful activities of trade. " I believe," said Lord Salisbury in 1871, "that since the Declaration of Paris the fleet, valuable as it is for preventing an invasion of these shores, is almost valueless for any other purpose." He forgot its value in assisting our own oversea operations and in protecting the oversea communications of our commerce, but, subject to these qualifications, his judgment was, broadly, sound. Some of those who agreed with him were for denouncing the Declaration of Paris, and for going back to the old rules of the Napoleonic Wars ; others agreed that as the powers of our fleet over the enemy's commerce had been so reduced, the right course was to give up rights of capture, which were worthless used against a continental enemy, and might be dangerous used against an island Power like our-selves. The one section said : " You cannot afford, as a naval Power, to respect this encroachment of neutral privilege on belligerent rights." The other said : " You cannot go back to Napoleonic practice ; it is dangerous to stand still ; the best course is to make a virtue of necessity, and to proclaim the freedom of the seas by abolishing the right of capture of all enemy property except contraband." The outbreak of the war found the Government halting dubiously between these two voices.

The Declaration of London, not having been ratified by Parliament, was not binding in this country, and we were therefore free to repudiate it. There were, however, difficulties in doing so, because, though not ratified, it had been signed, and it was, after all, only by a mere technicality of constitutional law, because the International Prize Courts proposed to be set up would supersede the authority of English Prize Courts, that the consent of Parliament was necessary to its validity. The Treaty guaranteeing the neutrality of Belgium had not been ratified by Parliament either. Having made this Treaty the main ground of our intervention, and denounced the Chancellor for describing it as a " scrap of paper," it was not easy to proceed to treat the Declaration of London as a " scrap of paper." Neither, having entered on the war for the defence of neutral rights, was it easy to begin by withdrawing the rights guaranteed to neutrals and non-combatants by the Declaration of London. The Allies, there- fore, decided to observe the provisions of the Declaration subject to one modification : that the enemy was not to be free to import through neutral ports articles of conditional contraband destined for belligerent use. This modification, however, did not materially strengthen our belligerent power. We drove the enemy's fleet off the seas, not, however, without suffering losses which were at any rate commensurate with the enemy's losses through the laying up of his ships in port. There was some restriction in the enemy's supplies, not through our blockade—for as a blockade of Germany was useless without a blockade of Holland, which was impossible, we had not troubled to declare one—but through the scarcity of shipping. But the economic strangulation of Germany, so far from tightening, was hardly beginning.

Nor could it have begun if Germany had kept as legally within the law as the Allies had done. With a folly that has rarely been equalled in the conduct of war, she proceeded to supply us with cumulative justification for a strangulation that would otherwise have been impossible. She sowed mines indiscriminately in the high seas, and the narrow escape off the north of Ireland of a great liner was followed as a measure of retaliation by the closing of the North Sea except for a channel in the Straits. Germany in turn retaliated by the proclamation of her submarine blockade, which we answered by placing a complete embargo on all German commerce, inward and outward, through her own or through neutral ports. The policy of the Tirpitz faction—a policy which there is reason to believe was resisted, though in vain, by the Chancellor and the Moderates—thus gave us what nothing else could have given, the opportunity of establishing a complete blockade of German over-sea trade, whether through her own or neutral ports. If Germany had observed the rules of war her ports would have been open for the importation of all the articles on the free list, including cotton. Even conditional contraband would have been imported through her own and neutral ports unless it could be proved that it was for belligerents and not for purely commercial use. And had we attempted to extend our rights farther, we could only have done so by imitating at sea that gross invasion of treaty rights which Germany had committed on land by forcing her passage through Belgium. Those advantages German policy deliberately threw away.

Meanwhile, German diplomacy had been busy in the United States. It is a fixed belief with nearly all Englishmen that British naval power is an instrument of liberty ; the phrase " maritime tyranny " is, to their minds, a patent self-contra-diction. That, however, is not a universal view, nor is it the view generally held in the United States. Ever since Benjamin Franklin's days it has been the policy of the American Government to press for the abolition of the right of capture at sea. It holds that this right is as offensive to public morality as the taking of booty in land operations. Throughout her chief opponent in securing this reform has been Great Britain. Nor was America's advocacy of this reform an example merely of devotion to principle. Before the Civil War her merchant marine was second only to ours, and to build up another great merchant fleet has long been one of the objects of the Democratic party. But the law of capture, it was believed in America, made it impossible for a nation to retain its merchant marine in war-time unless it had also an overwhelming naval supremacy over its opponent ; and her politicians resented rules' of war which exposed an inferior naval Power to this penalty. Moreover, there was a long history of quarrel between England and the United States on our exercise of belligerent rights against neutrals at sea. Nor did the United States take the British view of the political uses to which our naval power has been put in the past. The attitude of the average friendly American to British naval power was and is very much like that of the advanced English Liberal in the middle of the nineteenth century. Take, for example, the following passage from Professor Beesly's essay on " England and the Sea," and we shall not be far from the attitude of mind of the average American now. It does not invalidate the argument that when Professor Beesly wrote France was still the traditional enemy, and that his essay was a plea for better relations between this country and the great nation that is now its ally :—

Suppose Napoleon I had left France a great naval Power, in possession of Portland, the Isle of Man, and the Aland Isles ; suppose one Fleet permanently cruised off the mouth of the Mersey and another in the Baltic ; does any one imagine that England and the Northern Powers would ever be brought to look on such a state of things as natural or tolerable ? If it dated from Louis XIV, would a century and a half have reconciled us to it ? Would a dozen treaties and peaces have made it sacred in our eyes? Should we excuse it on the ground of an extensive commerce, numerous colonies, or the police of the seas? Englishmen, I think, would then understand very well the meaning of the phrase "maritime tyranny," which they now profess themselves unable to comprehend.

The average American, in fact, was at the beginning of this war prepared to think of British naval power much as the Englishman thinks of German military power. Take each of the charges brought against German militarism, and it does not require much ingenuity to find a parallel in the history of British "navalism." The German military theory is to wage war in the enemy's territory. It is the British naval theory too. German military power has set at naught the rights of neutral Powers. British naval power has done the same in past history. The bombardment of Copenhagen by Nelson is a rough parallel (though not one to be pressed) to the invasion of Belgium. German militarism is cruel to non-combatants. But does a naval blockade, in its intention at any rate, restrict to combatants the suffering that it causes? Is not starvation by cutting off supplies an equally efficient and more economical way of killing babies than by bombarding them with 12-in. naval guns or dropping incendiary bombs from Zeppelins? Is there much difference, so far as the victim is concerned, between the lawless looting of German officers on land and the confiscation of private property at sea by British officers in accordance with processes of law which the British Government has persistently refused to amend? Such sentiments, though they appear shocking and perverse to the average Englishman, occur quite naturally to the average American. That it should be so postulates a state of mind that is a permanent danger to relations of active and cordial friendship between this country and the United States. And how great that danger is may be inferred from the fact that not all the inhumanity of German submarine policy, the murder of American citizens on the high seas, the repeated flouting of American dignity, were able to obliterate in the mind of the average American the idea that there was no essential difference between German militarism and British navalism, that the one was tyranny on land and the other tyranny at sea. To Englishmen, Germany's claim that she was contending for the freedom of the seas seems merely impudent and perverse, especially when it is put forward in a dispatch replying to American protests against the killing of American citizens travelling by the *Lusitania*. Yet President Wilson took it quite seriously. In his third *Lusitania* dispatch he wrote :—

" The Government of the United States and the Imperial German Government, contending for the same great object, long stood together in urging the very principles on which the Government of the United States now insists. They are both contending for the freedom of the seas. The Government of the United States will continue to contend for that freedom without compromise and at any cost. It invites the practical co-operation of the Imperial German Government at this time, when

co-operation may accomplish much and this great
common object can be most strikingly and effec-
tively achieved.   The Imperial German Government express the hope that this object may be
accomplished even before the present war ends.
It can be.   The Government of the United States
not only feels obliged to insist upon it, by whom-
soever it is violated or ignored, in the protection
of its own citizens, but it is also deeply interested
in   seeing   it   made   practicable   between   the
belligerents themselves.   It holds itself ready at
any time to act as a common friend who may
be privileged to suggest a way."

In spite of the outrage of sinking the *Lusitania*,
President Wilson is still ready to give Germany
credit for desiring the freedom of the seas and
still remembers the early treaty with Prussian
Frederic, guaranteeing exemption of the private
property of Americans and Prussians from the
operations   of   war   between   their   countries.
Germany, in spite of her terrible works, was
saved from utter disgrace in American eyes by
that old faith in the freedom of the seas which
she still professed.   England's works might be
less heinous and even relatively good ; but the
faith was not in her.   And so in spite of the great
consideration shown by this country for the interests
of the United States and the woeful lack of respect
for the United States and for ordinary humanity
shown by Germany, the two countries are treated
by the United States as equally at fault.   And
in pari delicto potior est conditio defendentis.
From which it may be inferred how dangerous

would have been the relations between this country
and the United States if Germany had not, with
a stupidity cloaked but not concealed by her inhumanity, deliberately put herself in the wrong
by sowing mines broadcast and by torpedoing
merchantmen on the high seas for no offence
known to international law or morality.

No doubt the difficulties of our position were
exaggerated by the somewhat unfortunate methods
of retaliation adopted by this country.   We could
have secured precisely the same results by de-
claring a blockade of German ports, by extending
the doctrine of continuous voyage so as to cover
imports of contraband and quasi-contraband
through neutral ports by Germany, and, lastly, if
these steps were insufficient, by extending our list
of contraband.   Mr. Asquith's announced intention not to allow our embargo to be embarrassed
by "juridical niceties" hardly became a nation
which was defending the idea of law in international affairs.   The law cannot be distinguished
from the forms which he proposed quite unneces-
sarily to set aside.   But whatever our Government had done, there would have been great difficulty in extending our belligerent rights so as to
deal Germany a really serious blow.   The broad
fact is that but for Germany's violations of the
law she might have escaped all serious injury to
her economic life from the operations of our fleet,
except such as was inseparable from the scarcity
of shipping and from the cessation of the earnings
of her great shipping companies.   Every outrage
committed by Germany at sea was the occasion of

a fresh accession of power to the British fleet which it would not otherwise have acquired. But even so, when Von Tirpitz had done the best for the British Navy and the worst for his own country by his blunders, it may be doubted whether the British Navy by its war on German commerce appreciably shortened the war or indeed inflicted much more injury on Germany than our own shipping received. " If we look at the example of former periods," said Lord Palmerston in a speech explaining the Declaration of Paris to the Liverpool Chamber of Commerce, " we shall not find that any powerful country was ever vanquished through the losses of individuals. It is the conflict of armies by land and of fleets by sea that decides the great contests of nations."

To sum up, the conclusions so far reached are these : First, if no injury had been done to the trade of neutrals, the British Navy would have been powerless to inflict more than inconvenience on the economic life of Germany—an inconvenience trifling by comparison with that caused by the mobilization of the Army. Secondly, even after Germany's violation of the laws of war and of the rights of neutrals had led to the retaliatory embargo on all German trade, it is doubtful whether the war of our fleet on private commerce has had any appreciable effect on the duration of the war. Thirdly, whatever conclusions may be drawn from this war must hold with redoubled force of any other conceivable war. The Germanic Allies in this war are islanded in European conflict. Of all the countries of Europe which have a seaboard and interior communications with Germany only five—Roumania, Norway and Sweden, Denmark and Holland—are neutral. In no other possible war could the proportion of neutral coastline to the area affected by the war be so small. It is obvious that a war on German commerce with France as a neutral or on France with Germany as a neutral would be impracticable. We could not blockade a great and powerful neutral country ; yet without such blockade our Navy could hardly touch the enemy's oversea commerce. The damage to the enemy's commerce by our naval operations is therefore greater in this than it could be in any other conceivable war, and if it is small in this war, it would be quite negligible in any other. On the other hand, if the injury of a commercial blockade against a continental country is to amount to anything, it can only do so at the cost of injury to neutrals and to the prejudice of our politics in regard to them. In a sentence, the seas are too free for the exercise of really effectual naval war on commerce, not free enough to satisfy neutrals or to establish the British Navy as the acknowledged champion of international law and equity at sea. As Englishmen of all shades of political opinion have agreed, from Cobden to Mr. Gibson Bowles, from Bright to Mr. F. E. Smith, we must go forward or backward. The law cannot remain suspended between the ancient and the modern worlds as it was when this war broke out.

Although the blunders of Von Tirpitz had

enabled this country to go back a century in its practice and to wage this war on rules even stricter than those of the Napoleonic days, a permanent practice cannot be founded on the abnormal and transient justification of German excesses. The alternative policy of going forward merits a closer examination. What are we to understand by the phrase " the freedom of the seas "? It will not do to say that it means freedom for Germany to do as she pleases, for as the quotation already made from President Wilson's dispatches shows, it is possible to approve of the idea even while protesting against Germany's right to do as she pleases. Moreover, Sir Edward Grey has himself declared that the idea may well form the subject of negotiation when the war is over.

By the freedom of the seas is meant the exemption of commerce from the operations of war so long as it does not take part in them. This exemption is to apply to the commerce of belligerent as well as of neutral countries ; and the proviso that the exemption is forfeited if commerce takes a part in military operations contemplates as a necessary corollary an exacter and probably a wider definition of contraband by international agreement. There is no freedom so long as enemy's private property is liable to capture at sea under its own flag ; and the phrase therefore at the least implies the acceptance of the reform which the United States have persistently advocated since Franklin's day. But the principle may imply more. It may be found on examination to involve the abolition of commercial as distinguished from naval blockade. This distinction would need very careful working out in detail, but two tests have been suggested: "First, if a port is a naval arsenal or is sheltering the ships of the enemy, its blockade is a naval operation and is permissible. Secondly, if a port, though not an arsenal or a place of arms, is being used as a basis for the operations of the hostile fleet, or if it is invested by land by an armed force and the blockade may be held to be a completion by sea of the siege lines, in such case again the blockade is permissible. Non-combatants may suffer from such blockade, but their suffering is incidental to the scheme of military operations and not its whole or main object, as in commercial blockade proper." [1] This, then, is the complete conception of the freedom of commerce on the seas, as understood by Cobden ; but inability to accept the whole would not preclude this country, if it saw fit, from accepting a part. The United States would certainly be willing to accept a part.

The principles underlying such proposals for securing the freedom of the seas are broad and simple, and correspond somewhat closely with the heads of our quarrel with German militarism. German militarism is accused, and justly, of violating the rights of neutrals. But we have seen that any naval war on commerce, if it is to be effective, must necessarily interfere with neutral

[1] "The Freedom of Commerce in War." By Mancunian. A pre-war pamphlet issued by the National Reform Union.

rights of trade. It takes two to make a bargain—
that is to say, to trade ; and any interference with
the trade of one party is necessarily an interference
with the trade of the other, and this other (trade
between belligerents being suspended by war)
is always a neutral. It would seem, therefore, to follow that our advocacy of the rights of
neutrals in land warfare requires as its com-
plement the advocacy of their rights on the sea.
Secondly, German militarism is accused of neglect-
ing the distinction between combatant and non-
combatant subjects of the enemy belligerent. To
some extent, the confiscation of enemy property at
sea does the same. Looting on land is forbidden by
law ; on sea it is sanctioned by law, but ought, if
this principle of distinguishing between combatants and non-combatants is to be enforced, to
be prohibited. Again, the abolition of the right
of capture would in effect internationalize three-
quarters of the surface of the globe and place
it under the rule of law. *Ego terræ dominus lex
maris*, in Justinian's phrase. There is some in-
compatibility between our denunciation of Germany's preponderant military strength as a menace
to Europe and our assertion of our right to
form a Navy double the strength of any other.
Lastly, what is the radical vice of ·German
militarism which we are combating but its denial
of all individual and private rights where these
conflict with the will of the State? It insists on
war being a relation, not between State and State,
but ·between the individuals composing the States.
Articles 33-6 of the Declaration of London, in

laying down the rules of conditional contraband,
draw a distinction between civilian and State uses
of an article of import.   How can that distinction
be kept up in dealing with a State which when
it is at war claims the life and services of every
one without distinction?   Even in England it has
become a commonplace that every one is a combatant, if not in the firing line then in the munitions
workshop, and if not in the workshop then
at his private work, increasing the taxable wealth
of the country.   The system which the necessities
of the war has forced upon England is part of the
permanent organization of the State in Germany,
and this is what we understand by " continental
militarism."   It is not reasonable that Germany,
who maintains this system on land, and forces
her neighbours to adopt it, too, should claim to
enforce the rival system on the other element.
As against Germany, we are fully justified in
maintaining the full vigour of " navalism " as a
counterpoise to her militarism.   But such a
counterpoise of evils is neither in our own nor
in the general interest.   There is a clear distinction
between the end and the means that we take to
the end.   The end, as set up by Mr. Asquith, is
the destruction of militarism.   The attainment of
that end necessarily implies, if we are sincere,
the abandonment of " navalism "—that is to say,
the complete immunity, so far as rules of war
can secure it, of neutrals and of non-combatants from the operations of naval war.   And
if this immunity would help us to secure the
overthrow of German militarism, we should not

wait till the end of the war to concede it or to promise to concede it.

The same conclusions may be reached by other directions of thought. If it be true that this war has made relations of closer friendship with the United States one of the first of our political necessities, the story of the negotiations between the United States and Germany has revealed the freedom of the seas as an indispensable condition of that closer friendship. It may be, too, that just as the war on land has shown the excesses of German militarism to be not only crimes but blunders, so, too, the full history of the war will show that our attempts to wage war on German commerce have not materially influenced its progress, but have caused us as much loss as we have inflicted. These arguments, however, may be developed with more certainty when the complete story of the war is before us. But though they may, and probably will, confirm conclusions reached by the argument based on political principle and international justice, they cannot in any case invalidate them.

THE
OPEN
DOOR

THE OPEN DOOR

By J. A. HOBSON

THERE can be no security of durable peace unless the chief economic causes of discord among nations are removed. For though the conscious motives which incite nations to prepare for war and to engage in it may be self-defence, the claims of nationality, the sentiments of liberty and of humanity, the maintenance of public law, behind these motives always lies the pressure of powerful economic needs and interests. It is idle to seek to determine the relative strength and importance of these economic and non-economic factors. We need not accept the cynical maxim that " all modern wars are for markets " in order to realize the part which commerce and finance play in fomenting international disputes. But history makes it manifest that at all times the contacts and conflicts between different nations are chiefly due to the attempts of members of one nation, or tribe, or other group, to seek its livelihood or gain beyond the confines of its own country. Migrations or plundering raids, conducted under the pressure of congested population and scarcity of food, impulsive overflows from thickly peopled into sparsely peopled areas, were chief causes of strife among primitive peoples, and must still be regarded as the deepest underlying sources of disturbance in many parts of the world. The large highly organized commerce of modern times, taken in conjunction with extractive and manufacturing arts that enable vastly increased yields of foods and other material requisites of life to be got from restricted areas of land, greatly abates the force of these violent overflows. But this commercial intercourse between nations makes the inhabitants of every country far more dependent upon persons and events outside the area of their own country than was formerly the case. This divergence between political and economic areas of interest and control is of the first significance in understanding our problem. It enables us to perceive a certain unreality or inadequacy in the stress laid upon " nationality " or " political autonomy " as the basis of a satisfactory settlement. No measure of political independence, however complete, could secure for any moderately progressive people the freedom which they require. For every people needs access to the produce and the markets of other peoples, the right to buy and sell abroad on reasonable terms. The idea of an economically self-contained State has long been obsolescent. Though militarist States have sometimes grasped and even realized the possibility of reverting to a self-sufficing economic basis during a period of war, the normal life of every modern nation rests upon a basis of large and expanding opportunities outside its political area.

Every modern industrial nation, with a large and growing population, demands that its Government shall assist it in securing and maintaining ample liberties and opportunities of access to the economic resources of other countries. It seeks three economic liberties. First comes liberty of trade, the right of access for its traders and manufacturers to buy and sell in foreign markets without excessive or oppressive barriers in the shape of tariffs, tolls, fines, or other obstacles or prohibitions. As a country becomes more thickly peopled, and so tends to specialize more closely upon certain productive occupations especially adapted to its natural resources, its working population, and its situation, it becomes more and more dependent for some of its essentials of livelihood upon external supplies. So far as foreign trade is conducted between the members of civilized nations, the mutual advantages of such exchange afford a strong, though not always a sufficiently strong, basis for free intercourse. Cobden was not wrong when he insisted that the reciprocal gains of free interchange of goods formed a genuine guarantee of peace. How, then, does it come to pass that most civilized nations have since sought to place irksome restrictions upon this intercourse, and that a diagnosis of most modern wars shows that the chief directing motive is a pressure for markets? No adequate answer to this question is possible, until account is taken of the growing importance of the economic relations of civilized with uncivilized or undeveloped countries. For it is in their dealings with these backward countries that trade invites economic and political interference, and evokes international antagonism.   Though political considerations, missionary enterprise, and other activities of an adventurous people, appreciably affect these dealings, colonization and imperial expansion are essentially economic processes.   They originate from simple trade.

For the successful conduct of trade, casual visitations of merchant vessels needed to be supplemented by permanent settlements, with a view to the orderly collection of goods and the application of the stimuli, inducements, or pressures needed to get natives to perform the necessary work and to acquire the habits of consuming the articles of foreign barter.   So the foreign land and labour fall more and more under white men's control, and the cultivation of sugar, coffee, tobacco, and other crops supplements the earlier rude processes of barter and collection. Roads, harbours, and other large permanent works must be undertaken, and permanent government, half economic, half political, set on foot.   Exploitation of the mineral and other natural resources leads to organized arrangement for their profitable working.   Large capital is invested in mines and railways, and in cities suited to the requirements of white officials and business men.

Two important changes have now come to pass. Simple trade between the peoples of the two countries is no longer the chief consideration.   The backward country has become an area of profitable exploitation and investment.   Development and investment companies supplement and direct the trading interests, and financial schemes for operating gold mines, rubber and tea plantations, and for building railroads, are hatched by little groups of financiers in London, Paris, or Berlin. The country is now primarily an area for investment, not a mere outlet for the sale of goods. The two processes, of course, are intimately related, for invested capital goes out chiefly in the form of goods, the engines, rails, mining plant, and other stores which the developing process requires. But financiers are henceforth in chief control, and monetary operations control the fate of the country thus " penetrated." This economic change affects political relations. White traders and manufacturers have always utilized the services of their Governments to procure access to foreign markets, sometimes by force of arms, as in the case of the Opium War with China. But as soon as a backward country has become an area of investment, political interference is apt to be more exigent. The processes of economic development involve the presence of white managers, engineers, and other " outlanders," as well as the control of native labour and various interferences with native habits. Native unrest discloses a government incompetent to the protection of life and property. The white man's government must intervene, and a " sphere of interest " passes into a protectorate, whose political control is apt to become tighter in accordance with the needs of the economic situation, as interpreted by financiers at home and " men upon the spot." Though other political and genuinely humanitarian tendencies commingle with the economic drive of events, the latter, being consciously exercised by business men with a clear view of what they want, is the determinant factor. The recent history of colonial and imperial development on the part of European Powers everywhere furnishes a convincing demonstration of the powerful secret, or occasionally open, direction of foreign policy by financial and commercial interests working in sympathy with political aspirations. Egypt, the Transvaal, Morocco, Tripoli, Persia, Mexico, China afford recent illustrations of this direction of foreign policy by capitalist interests. The process finds, of course, its most refined expression in the struggles of rival banking groups within the several capitalistic countries to finance the Governments of Russia, Persia, or China and to use their respective Foreign Offices to push their profitable projects.

From the standpoint of the developed economic nation with great reserves available for foreign trade and investment, and with growing dependence upon foreign sources of supply, the political-economic process here described appears under the guise of economic liberty. This will be evident from our British outlook, for we have gone so much farther along this road than any other nation. Our effective " freedom," the opportunity to satisfy our needs and tastes, to supply ourselves with the requisite variety of foods and other articles for our progressive standards of life, to procure the goods necessary to sustain our industries and to promote our material prosperity, rests upon free, large, regular, and growing access to the resources of other lands and upon full opportunities to assist in their discovery and development. In this we need " freedom of the sea," or safe conduct for our merchant ships over the waters of the world, the right of entry into foreign ports, " freedom of trade " in the sense of the secure use of trade routes and markets upon equal terms with other foreigners, and " freedom of investment," or the equal right to assist in the profitable development of countries which are in need of capital. In proportion as we are restricted in any of these opportunities we suffer a loss of economic liberty, which in the last resort might mean a loss of life itself. What holds of Great Britain holds in different degrees of all other developed or developing peoples. Their effective freedom requires free outlets and equal opportunities beyond the confines of their own political area.

Associated with the claims for equal opportunities for commerce and investment is the claim for freedom of migration. If capital is properly to play its part in developing sparsely peopled countries, labour should be free to enter them. *Laissez-aller* is demanded alike in the interests of capital and of labour. Every restriction upon the free flow of labour from thickly into thinly populated lands, from lower-waged into higher-waged areas, is *prima facie* an interference with the liberty of workers to improve their conditions and with the best development of the world's resources. As knowledge of economic opportunities and facilities of transport are enlarged, this liberty of migration is more highly valued, and its denial or restriction is a more frequent and graver source of international friction.

These economic liberties of trade, investment, and migration, which are so essential to the prosperity or even the existence of certain industrially advanced or over-populated countries, are unfortunately found to conflict with the " rights " of the rulers or inhabitants of other countries whom these liberties affect. By tariffs, bounties, or prohibitions, goods are refused free admittance to profitable markets ; trade routes by land or sea are barred ; legal restrictions are put upon the acquisition or use of land or the control of industries by foreign capital and management ; monopolies or privileges are assigned by favour, corruption, or political " pull " ; alien laws preclude the introduction 'of the necessary supplies of labour. Everywhere " liberties " of economic expansion claimed by some nations are confronted by " liberties " of exclusion claimed by others.

These conflicts of " liberty " underlie the armed preparations and the wars of the modern world. In order to give point to what otherwise may seem a vague generality, I will cite an interesting analysis of the deeper causes of the present war as they present themselves to thoughtful business men in a neutral country [1] :—

Consider the situation of the present belligerents :—

Serbia wants a window on the sea, and is shut out by Austrian influence.

[1] Memorandum of the Reform Club of New York.

Austria wants an outlet in the East, Constantinople or Salonika.

Russia wants ice-free ports in the Baltic and Pacific, Constantinople, and a free outlet from the Black Sea into the Mediterranean.

Germany claims to be hemmed in by a ring of steel, and needs the facilities of Antwerp and Rotterdam for the Rhine Valley commerce, security against being shut out from the East by commercial restrictions in the overland route, and freedom of the seas for her foreign commerce.

England must receive uninterrupted supplies of food and raw materials, and her oversea communications must be maintained.

This is also true of France, Germany, Belgium, and other European countries.

Japan, like Germany, must have opportunity for her expanding population, industries, and commerce.

The foreign policies of the nations still at peace are also determined by trade relations. Our own country desires the open door in the East.

South and North American States and Scandinavia are already protesting against the war's interference with their ocean trade.

All nations that are not in possession of satisfactory harbours on the sea demand outlets, and cannot and ought not to be contented till they get them.

Nations desiring to extend their colonial enterprises entertain these ambitions for commercial reasons, either to possess markets from which they cannot be excluded, or to develop such markets for themselves, and be able to exclude others from them when they so determine.

If any reasonably safe basis of settlement is to be found, some reconciliation of these opposing " liberties " must be discovered. To some thinkers, reared in the older school of economic harmonies,

salvation lies in the removal of all political and
legal restrictions, and a reversion of the Foreign
Offices of all countries to a policy of non-inter-
vention. It is with them a plain and simple
application of the principles of individual liberty.
It should, they hold, be possible to convince the
peoples and Governments of every country that
their advantage lies in admitting on terms of
absolute equality the trade, the capital, the labour-
power of other countries, and in giving foreigners
every facility for assisting in the development of
the national resources. In this utmost extension of
economic internationalism the greatest prosperity
of the world and of each constituent nation will
be found. Though traders and investors are
primarily out for private gain, and not for any
increase of the wealth of their nation or of the
world, their enterprise will incidentally, but necessarily secure the wider economic welfare. It must,
however, be objected that the principles and practices of most highly developed States are so
strongly committed to fiscal Protection and to other
uses of political power for the furtherance of
foreign trade, as to render any early hope of an
acceptance of complete economic liberty chimerical.
The financial position of every belligerent country
after this war must render any lowering of tariffs,
involving sacrifice of revenue, impracticable, to say
nothing of the strong disposition to seek present
security, at the expense of opulence, in closer
national self-sufficiency. It will, I think, be recognized that the war will have checked for the time
being the movement towards Free Trade among the

developed nations which was discernible in recent
years, and that its renewal will depend upon the
necessarily slow process of establishing general
confidence in arrangements for a pacific future.

If, then, liberty and equality of economic opportunities form an essential of any lasting settlement,
the early application of the policy must lie in agreements for the commercial and financial development
of extra-European countries and markets.   Supposing that the eight Great Powers, together with the
smaller developed European countries, could come
to an agreement for the equal admission of their
trade and capital to all colonial possessions, protectorates, or spheres of influence, present or prospective, not merely would the gravest causes of
future antagonism be removed, but substantial new
bonds of community of international interest would
be provided.

" World-power," " place in the sun," " freedom
of the seas "—the three phrases which inspire the
aggressive policy of Germany—derive most of the
potency of their appeal from the sense of constric-
tion which German industrial and commercial men
experienced as they sought new outlets in the world
for their produce, their capital, and their enterprises.   Prussian militarism, the doctrines of
Treitzschke and Bernhardi, the expansive claims of
German " Kultur," would have been ineffective had
they not been supported by the feeling of restricted
enterprise and thwarted ambition which led large
numbers of the business men to support the *Flotten
Verein* and the pushful foreign policy it indicated.
Though the language of *Welt-politik*, of course,

had its appeal to the sentimental patriot in terms of territory and of political aggrandizement, expanding markets and profits were the *leit-motif* in German as in other imperialism. This war is for Germany in its essence a great economic project, designed to break down the barriers which impeded what her business classes deemed the legitimate expansion of their enterprise. Late in achieving industrial development on modern lines, Germany found herself forestalled in all parts of the New World suitable for genuine colonization, and in most of the tropical or sub-tropical lands with known rich resources and available supplies of native labour. As her industries came to yield larger surpluses for export trade, and her needs of foreign supplies of foods and materials became more urgent, this lack of the preferential markets, with which other competing industrial nations had provided themselves in their colonies and protectorates, and the fears lest the growing intensity of competition should close to them the open markets of the British Empire, served to whet her resentment against the existing arrangements, and were a formidable weapon in the hands of aggressive militarism.

It will no doubt be said that such an interpretation of their situation was a foolish one. Germany was, in fact, advancing in industrial development and in wealth faster than any other nation ; her foreign trade, based on cheapness, on quality, and on skilful marketing, was rapidly expanding, and she had no serious grounds for fearing any check upon her prosperity. No people ought to have been able to realize more fully the truth of the saying that you do not need to own a country in order to trade profitably with it. Are Germans, then, the victims of a mere illusion, to the effect that imperialism is a commercially profitable career for a nation? If they are, it is an illusion shared by all the other nations which have embarked upon the policy of territorial aggrandizement. Great Britain is sated with empire, mainly the result of pushful trading ; France, Italy, Holland believe themselves to derive great commercial advantages from their colonies ; economic exploitation has underlain the recent experiments of Japan and the United States in the acquisition of oversea territory.

To dispel an illusion so widely prevalent and so firmly held will not prove an easy enterprise. The first step towards doing so is to recognize in what sense it is and in what sense it is not an illusion. When a powerful civilized State annexes or assumes political control over an undeveloped country in Africa, or a group of Pacific islands, securing internal order and enabling white traders and planters to live there safely and conduct their business, it is generally true that this enlargement of economic opportunities brings an increase of wealth for the world at large. It is also usually the case that the lion's share of these economic gains, whether in the shape of trade or of lucrative investment, falls to members of the nation which has taken on the work of " Empire." For, though the doctrine that " trade follows the flag " has been stated in an exaggerated form, it con-

tains a considerable element of truth even in cases
where political control is not avowedly used to
secure an exclusive or a preferential market.
Though Free Trade prevails throughout the British
Empire (with the exception of the self-governing
dominions), political dominion and prestige are
undoubtedly favourable to British trade and British
capital in the work of development which is carried
on. Imperialism everywhere proceeds by the
mutual support of politics and commerce. But
the recognition of the commercial utility of the flag
by no means implies that Imperialism is necessarily or normally a profitable economic policy for
the nation that pursues it. For the gains that
accrue to the nation as a whole, including the
advantages its trade enjoys over those enjoyed by
other trading nations, are usually more than
balanced by the expenses of government, including
the costs and risks, direct and indirect, of the
policy of Imperial aggrandizement. Even our
Empire, *prima facie* the most prosperous the world
has known, would almost certainly be found, by
any complete statement of the credit and debit
account, not to be a profitable business proposi-
tion. Certainly the expansion of the last generation, inclusive of the costs of acquiring, maintaining,
and defending the new territories, would be found
to have cost enormously more than any present or
prospective addition it brings to the wealth of
our nation. Regarded from the standpoint of a
nation, the whole policy of territorial expansion
and the forceful foreign policy which it involves
are bad business. But from the standpoint of

certain financial, commercial, and manufacturing interests within the nation it is good business. For the political and military risks and costs of this colonial and foreign policy fall upon the nation as a whole, while the advantages accrue to favoured individuals. So long, therefore, as groups of business men within each nation are permitted to use the diplomacy and the armed forces of their State to push their trade with foreign countries, to secure for them concessions, spheres of exploitation, and other business privileges, and to protect and improve the trade and investments which they may have established by their private enterprise for their private profit, these perilous conflicts of foreign policy are likely to be a fatal obstacle to any scheme of international settlement. The roots of this disease of imperial expansion, which has been poisoning the foreign policy of all the Great Powers, lie in the excessive political and economic power of modern capitalism. The only radical cure is the progress of democratic control within each nation. A genuinely self-governing nation would not permit its foreign relations to be determined by the pressure of a group of bankers, or of financiers and contractors, of shipowners and merchants, conspiring with ambitious, jealous, or suspicious statesmen and diplomatists to embark upon new, perilous, and expensive projects in countries which do not belong to them. The determinant acts of the foreign policy of every civilized State are secretly influenced, and usually governed, by the strong will and clear-sighted purpose of business men, who wish to make money for themselves by persuading other people into putting their money into projects for making railways, developing minerals, oil, rubber, nitrates, etc., in countries which are backward and destitute of capital. The powerful pressure of financial and commercial interests along these lines of foreign and colonial policy is, however, largely an economic necessity due to a distribution of wealth as between the various classes of the advanced nations which, by restricting the quantity of capital that can find profitable investment at home, drives too large a surplus to seek oversea investment. A distribution of wealth or income more favourable to the labouring population of each country would, by raising the national standard of consumption in the body of the people, afford employment to a larger capital in the staple industries at home, while at the same time it reduced the proportion of that surplus wealth in the shape of rents and profits which is automatically saved and accumulated in the hands of the capitalist class. The improved efficiency of the industrial classes, resulting from a better distribution of wealth, might indeed produce so large an increase of wealth as to maintain the aggregate of savings as large as before, but the increased demand for commodities exercised by the workers would keep a larger share of the new capital at home, and would so proportionately relieve the pressure of that competition for foreign areas of investment which we see to be the economic root of international discord.

Peace in the future cannot be secured without

some such advance in the arts of political and economic democracy as shall release the foreign policy of the several nations from the control of private interests engaged in pushing for profitable markets, concessions, and spheres of business interests, and in lending money to or providing armaments for foreign Governments.

But, it will be said, this progress in fully enlightened popular government within each State must be a slow process. Meantime what lines of safety can be laid down for the present abatement of economic conflicts?

The proposal that Governments shall agree to a simple policy of " Hands off," leaving their " nationals " free to undertake any foreign trade or investments and work of development they choose entirely at their own discretion and their own risk, is quite impracticable.

An agreement of the Powers to proceed no farther with the policy of political absorption of backward countries, and with the political assistance hitherto given to private businesses for purposes of trade and finance, could furnish no possible basis for a pacific future. For, since most of the desirable areas of profitable exploitation have already been appropriated, and are in actual process of economic absorption, no equality of opportunity could be provided by an arrangement that would divide the Powers into two groups, one satisfied, the other unsatisfied, and would preclude the latter for ever from obtaining satisfaction. Great Britain, and, perhaps, France, already gorged with Empire, might be willing to assent to such a compact, but could Germany be expected to do so? Could Russia or Japan?

No less impracticable would the proposal be as applied to the unabsorbed portion of the earth. The notion that the Governments of the civilized States could safely or advantageously leave the further processes of economic development to the free play of private profiteering enterprise among their trading and financial classes must be rejected as soon as its meaning is realized. Such a policy of naked *laissez-faire* is quite inadmissible. A deliberate acceptance of the theory that bands of armed buccaneers calling themselves traders are free to rob defenceless savages, to poison them with alcohol or opium, to seize their lands, impose forced labour, and establish a slave trade is inconceivable. Such *laissez-faire* would soon convert any rich, unabsorbed corner of the world into a Congo, a San Thomé, or a Putumayo, tempered only by the fears of native risings and massacres. The mere abstinence from political intervention on the part of civilized States would plunge every unappropriated country into sheer anarchy. But, even if the Governments or peoples of certain undeveloped countries were able successfully to resist the entrance of foreign trade and capital, and to refuse all access to strangers, this is not a policy in which other peoples, or their Governments, can or ought to acquiesce. No reasonable interpretation of rights of nationality or independence can justify the inhabitants of a country in refusing both themselves to develop the resources of the country and to permit others to do so. Such absolute *jus*

utendi et abutendi is no more defensible as a right
of national property than it is of individual.   The
wandering tribes of hunters or herdsmen who may
form the sparse population of fertile lands, capable
of sustaining large settled communities and con-
tributing richly to the wealth and welfare of
surrounding nations, cannot be permitted to
practise a policy of permanent exclusion.   The
deposits of nitrates, rubber, copper, or other world-
wealth which they contain the world has a right
to insist shall not remain unutilized.

The problem is twofold : first, how to secure
the reasonable rights of the inhabitants of such
undeveloped countries against a policy of plunder,
extinction of life, or servitude imposed by the
people of a powerful aggressive State ; secondly,
how to secure equal opportunities to the members
of various advanced nations to participate in the
work of developing the natural resources and the
trade of these backward countries.

History shows that the former issue, primarily
one of justice and humanity, is intimately bound
up with the latter, the more distinctively economic,
issue.   The peace of the world is dependent upon
both.   The most ruthless acts of annexation and
the most wasteful practices of exploitation have
been due to the policy of exclusive possession and
protection imposed by the Government of a
colonizing nation in the short-sighted interest of
particular groups of traders or syndicates of capi-
talists.   If the Governments of all civilized nations
would consent to give equal rights of commerce
and equal facilities of investment and develop-

mental work in their colonies and protectorates to members of all nations, this single agreement would go farther to secure a peaceful future for the world than any other measure, such as reduction of armaments, general arbitration, or guarantees of national integrity. For not only would it greatly diminish the resentment and envy with which the older colonizing Powers are regarded by rising Powers, such as Germany and Japan, but it would greatly modify all competition for further acquisition of territory. If business interests, nationally grouped, could no longer hope to gain by pressing through their Foreign and Colonial Offices for annexation, charters, and concessions, and exclusive or preferential trading terms, the chief grounds for suspicion and hostility between the Governments of the Great Powers would be removed. It might then be a comparatively easy matter for friendly Governments to agree among themselves what policy to adopt with regard to still unappropriated countries, where dangerous disorder might prevail, or where the joint interests of all civilized peoples justified some interference or control. One method would be the establishment of a joint international protectorate, exercised by a Commission appointed by the permanent International Council, or whatever body was entrusted with the execution of the Treaty of International Relations. Another would be the delegation of this duty of protection by this international authority to the Government of some single nation, where propinquity or other special circumstances rendered this course advisable. The prestige of such " imperialism " would not arouse much jealousy if the nationals of the Power exercising it enjoyed no commercial or other advantages save such incidental ones as were unavoidably associated with the flag. Moreover, such incidental gains could be fairly apportioned by an international policy which distributed this work of protection and control fairly among the Governments of the civilized nations.

Such are the general principles for the realization of the Open Door. If the civilized nations could be brought to assent to the early extension of complete Free Trade and other free economic opportunities in all their home and colonial possessions, this achievement of full economic internationalism would afford a complete security for peace among the great States. But granting, as we must, that the financial situation of all European nations after this war, to say nothing of the political antagonisms and the impulses towards national economic self-sufficiency, will render any early movement towards such Free Trade impossible, can we not aim and hope to secure such a measure of the Open Door as we have here indicated? As regards equality of opportunity in existing colonies and protectorates, there are two practical obstacles to be overcome. One is the preferential tariffs of our self-governing dominions, the other those of the French colonies and protectorates. Is either obstacle insuperable? Though fiscal arrangements lie completely within the rights of self-government enjoyed by our dominions, the closer imperial relations likely to result from this war ought to make it an easy matter to secure a withdrawal of preferences primarily conceived as favours to the Mother Country, especially when such withdrawal would open to them, as to us, certain liberties of trade with the possessions of other Powers at present withheld.

The colonial system of France is so deeply rooted in Protection as to present graver difficulties. But even they should not be insuperable in view of the great commercial compensations and financial economies which the establishment of an Open Door would secure to her. Her colonial markets form a small proportion of her oversea trade ; most of this she would probably retain under free competition by motives of affection, habit, and prestige. By assenting to what might appear some present sacrifice, she would secure herself against the positive loss of the equal right of entrance she has hitherto enjoyed into the colonies of Great Britain, Germany, and Holland, and she would avoid the expensive and perilous pressures towards a pushful colonial policy which her financiers and commercial classes have constantly exercised upon her Government.

The size and value of trade preferences in existing colonies and protectorates ought not to be able to bar acceptance of the Open Door if the essential importance of this policy is made apparent. Nor should the more definitely constructive application of the doctrine to the political control and the economic exploitation of backward countries not yet absorbed prove impracticable. For, if economic monopolies and preferences are once extracted, political imperialism becomes an empty shell, an illusion of quantitative power conceived in idle terms of area and population. Even if we suppose that some of the distinctively political and sentimental supports of colonialism and imperialism survive, they will be greatly weakened in their hold of foreign policy, and, lacking the pushful direction of the business man, will be unlikely to engender dangerous disputes. Once convert the Open Door into a genuinely constructive policy of international co-operation, for the peaceful development of the undeveloped resources of the world, administered by impartial internationally minded men in the interests of the society of nations and with proper regard to the claims of the inhabitants of backward countries, a political support will have been found for that great and complex but hitherto " ungoverned " system of economic internationalism which has come into being during recent generations. The dangerous collisions between the forces of political nationalism and of economic internationalism would thus be obviated, not by denial of the claims of the former but by the political control of the latter.

THE
PARALLEL
OF THE
GREAT
FRENCH WAR

THE PARALLEL OF THE GREAT FRENCH WAR

By IRENE COOPER WILLIS

> We are in a war of a peculiar nature. . . . It is with an *armed doctrine* that we are at war. . . . This new system . . . in France cannot be rendered safe by any art . . . it must be destroyed or—it will destroy all Europe.
>
> BURKE's "Letters on a Regicide Peace," 1796.

OVER a distance of a hundred and twenty years Burke's thundering phrases travel, in striking accord with the denunciations of the militarism of the enemy of the moment. The circumstances of the two great wars—the war with revolutionary France and the present war with Germany—have been regarded by many people, the Prime Minister [1] among them, as similar in their legal and moral aspects. Then, as now, it has been said, the war arose out of an attack upon Belgium, and the challenge was accepted by the reluctant and peace-loving Pitt exactly as it was accepted by Mr. Asquith and Sir Edward Grey in August 1914.[2] We are told that we fought France then

---

[1] Mr. Asquith's speech at Edinburgh, September 19, 1914.

[2] *The Times'* Literary Supplement review of "The War Speeches of William Pitt," May 27, 1915.

for the rights of small nations and for honour just as now we are fighting their latest assailant, Germany. Now, as then, it is said, European liberties are being threatened by a Power aiming at world-dominion and arrogating to herself the right to destroy treaties. Now again, it is declared, almost in Burke's language, there can be no peace until the militarism of the enemy is utterly destroyed.

The purpose of this chapter is not, however, to show the likeness in rhetorical onslaught upon the enemy between the war which we entered upon in 1793 and that which we are engaged in to-day. Such evidence would be more useful to a psychological survey of the literature of all wars, for which survey English newspapers and pamphlets belonging to the three European wars in which England has taken part in modern times provide ample material. In passing, it may be said that not one of the philippics by which English statesmen and English men of letters are now marshalling their countrymen against Germany has not done equally good service on previous occasions. Only in 1793 it was France under whose foot European liberties were being crushed, it was France against whose treason, blasphemy, and murder a holy war was being waged ; and in the Crimean War we were fighting Russia for the sake of civilization and Turkey, in espousing whose quarrel it was said that we were backing the cause of freedom and progress against tyranny and despotism.

But the object of these pages is to represent

the situation of that far-distant war with revolutionary France as much as possible in the light of its opening circumstances and as it was viewed by men who, on this question, differed from Burke.

To accept Burke's opinion, without reference to other contemporary opinions, is a real return to his attitude but not a real return to his times. If it is desirable to go back to previous wars in order to fortify our conviction of England's constant intervention on the side of righteousness, it is better to go back as completely as the records of history permit us to go.

The average reference to the war with France in 1793 is apt to neglect the various stages of its long-drawn-out fury. Its first justification is considered as identical with that which at last really sustained it, namely the necessity of defending England and of delivering Europe from the ambitions of an insatiable despot. It is forgotten what share the war itself had in promoting that despotism, and to what extent the European Powers were responsible for its alliance with the principles of 1789.

Historians of all political tempers agree in the conclusion that war with the revolutionary government of France, as undertaken by Austria and Prussia in 1792, far from weakening the influence of the Jacobins, on the contrary, did everything to establish their savage rule by enabling them to identify their authority with the defence of the country against invasion. Whether or not the worst revolutionary horrors were inspired by the panic of invasion and under the menace of the Duke of Brunswick's manifesto and his subsequent march upon Paris, it is certain that the national peril alone united the warring civil factions and brought about that Jacobin supremacy which so hideously perverted the original revolutionary principles. Napoleon himself hated the Jacobins, and the majority of Frenchmen, who were not Terrorists, bent beneath the Terror's abominable yoke for the same reason that the majority of the people in any country, so insulted, so surrounded by advancing armies, as France was, abandon internal differences, however vital, and, with a united front, face the enemy.

Most historians also agree that the violation of the neutrality of the Scheldt was not the cause but merely the occasion of England's entry into the war. Neither in its actual nature nor in its influence upon governmental and popular opinion can it be compared to Germany's recent violation of Belgium. It was a misdemeanour, not a crime.

If it was a crime, then we ourselves had been criminally guilty a few years previously, for in 1784 we had been quite willing that Austria should commit the same breach of treaty rights respecting the navigation of the Scheldt upon conditions that did not include any reference to Holland's wishes in the matter. Holland in 1793 did not appeal for our assistance, though it was reported that prayers were offered in some of her churches that she might be spared from being plunged into war. The letters from Lord Grenville to the British Minister at The Hague, in December 1792 and

January 1793,[1] show his anxiety lest the Dutch should not interpret the French decree opening the Scheldt as an act of aggression, and his recognition that, until they so interpreted it, he was in an uncomfortable position.

Still more, if it was a crime, the Napoleonic wars perpetuated it, for one of their indisputable results, paraded by England with every show of gratification, was the freeing of the navigation of all the great rivers of Europe.

That it was considered a misdemeanour of slight importance compared to the other grounds we had for wishing to take part in the war is shown by the fact that the French Ambassador's, M. Chauvelin's, written offer to Lord Grenville to negotiate concerning the Scheldt and to give an immediate pledge to be bound by the Belgians' wishes in the matter after the close of the war with Austria was ignored by the English Foreign Minister as irrelevant.

Refusal to negotiate, refusal to state clearly what were the causes of complaint and the satisfaction demanded, before assuming that the case of strict necessity for war had arrived, were, as Fox and the Opposition of that day so often urged, the strongest proof that the true cause of the war was not the specific aggressions (the opening of the Scheldt, the decree of November 19, 1792), but the necessity, already proclaimed by the continental Powers in such violent language, of interfering with the internal government of France and of restoring the Bourbon monarchy.

[1] Auckland MSS., vol. xxxv, 383, 469.

The French had no desire for war. That much is evident from the correspondence between Lord Grenville and M. Chauvelin, whose pacific intentions, though diplomatically tactless actions, led him to submit to innumerable slights from the Foreign Office rather than relinquish his endeavours to maintain peace, and is further evidenced by Robespierre's angry attack upon Brissot for not having avoided war.

Negotiations might, indeed, have proved a failure in the furious state of the times, amid the indignation and hatred naturally produced in England by the September massacres, and, above all, by the execution of Louis in January 1793, and, too, with that discordant Convention which in Paris, amid the uproar of a Revolution, was issuing inflated decrees and strutting with pride at the triumph of its armies over the invader.

But to have shown a disposition to negotiate would have exonerated England from the charge of being the aggressor, and, moreover, a definite statement of her case would have dissociated her from the purpose of the allied kings and would have cleared her from the suspicion that she was acting in any degree on their principles.

Those purposes, however, England cannot disavow, nor can she clear herself from that suspicion. The reason does not lie only in the fact that when the war had begun her ministers openly availed themselves of the arguments with which the party which Burke inspired had, since the outbreak of the Revolution, been inflaming people's minds

against France as the centre of a deadly and
infectious anarchy, but in the explicit official
declarations of the Government.   There is an
admission from Pitt himself (December 9, 1795)
that the war was undertaken to prevent the progress of French principles and to re-establish the
hereditary monarchy : " I certainly said that the
war was not, like others, occasioned by particular
insult, or the unjust seizure of territory, or the
like, but undertaken to repel usurpation, connected
with principles calculated to subvert all government." And this was the note of our declaration
after taking Toulon in November 1793 ; no other
object of the war other than the restitution of the
French monarchy was then mentioned.

What moved Pitt from his apparently inflexible
determination to preserve England's neutrality in
the war between France and the Allied Powers
cannot be referred to any single specific cause.
His own hatred of the Revolution had, it is true,
been openly expressed, but, in his ministerial
capacity, he, at first, saw little to fear and much
to gain from France's collapse as a Great Power,
and this conviction was for a time proof against
all the appeals on behalf of the safety of Louis,
the danger to the Austrian Netherlands, and the
moral considerations which Burke had for long
urged as an overwhelming case for war.   Nor
was our alliance with Prussia ever mentioned either
by Prussia or ourselves as a reason for our intervention, a fact which is in itself evidence that
Austria and Prussia knew very well that they were
the aggressors in 1792, since, by the terms of

that alliance, England was bound to give help to Prussia if the latter were attacked.

England's case against France was essentially a cumulative one, and a careful survey of all the circumstances admits of very little doubt that some, and not unimportant, determinants of Pitt's change of attitude must be sought in the state of political affairs in England, and in his desire to divide the Whigs and, above all, to break the power of his great rival, Charles James Fox. Pitt was one of the most consummate opportunists that ever dominated English politics. He played in 1792 and 1793 a stupendous game and, for his purposes, he enlisted the fear of the French Revolution which Burke was brandishing. Whether Pitt cared for power for its own sake or for the sake of his country's advancement, it is difficult to deny that in 1792 he was more concerned to compass the downfall of the Whigs and to strengthen himself in office than to avoid what he then considered an inevitable war with the French. The Court, aristocracy, and clergy were for war, the country was worked up to the pitch of accepting it, if necessary, and Pitt's personal preference for peace stood against the interests of his own party and his own position. War presented an opportunity of consolidating the latter and, at the same time, of creating a division among the Whigs whereby Fox's power would be permanently crippled, and Pitt seized the opportunity. His optimism concerning the probable short duration of the war no doubt made the venture seem less tremendous than we, looking back over those twenty-two years of almost incessant warfare, can pronounce it to be, and to his patriotic motives the following extract from *The Times* [1] of February 8, 1793, the day before the French declaration of war reached England, supplies a hint :—

"France is the only Power whose maritime force has hitherto been a balance to that of Great Britain and whose commerce has rivalled ours in the two worlds, whose intrigues have fomented and kept alive ruinous wars in India. Could England succeed in destroying the naval strength of her rival, could she turn the tide of 'that rich commerce which has so often excited her jealousy in favour of her own country, could she connect herself with the French establishments in either India, the degree of commercial prosperity to which these kingdoms would then be elevated would exceed all calculations. It would not be the work of a few years only but would require ages for France to recover to the political balance of Europe that preponderance which she enjoyed previous to the Revolution. Such is the point of view under which Governments ought to consider the commercial interests. The indispensable necessity of extinguishing the wide-spreading fire whose devouring flames will sooner or later extend over all Europe and the well-grounded confidence of disembarrassing the commerce of Great Britain from the impediments which have so often clogged its wheels—these reasons, added to the prospect of

[1] *The Times* then, as in 1914, supported the war policy of the Ministry.

annihilating the French marine, ought to determine us to immediate war."

Burke, whatever the grounds of his fanatical
devotion to aristocracy, was whole-hearted in his
hatred of the Revolution and in his indignation
at its excesses. Only his real conviction that the
English Constitution was in danger from a Jacobin
party in England, bent upon the same hideous
drama as was being enacted in Paris, made him
break with a party and a friend with whom he
had worked for years in close agreement and to
associate himself with Pitt, whose political measures
it had been that party's constant aim to combat.
His grounds for believing in the existence of
revolutionary conspiracy [1] were no sounder than
those upon which in the " Reflections upon the
French Revolution " he arraigned the principles
of 1789. The prophecy of that amazing pamphlet
was indeed to a great extent fulfilled, but the
temper which it and its author encouraged, in
England and on the Continent, had not a little to
do with the fulfilment.

[1] The value which ministers attached to this argument and,
at the same time, the difficulty of getting enough evidence to
substantiate it, is shown in the following extract from Lord
Grenville's letter to Lord Auckland in January 1793 : "We have
some idea of laying before a secret committee of the two
Houses (very small in number) some particulars of the designs
which have been in agitation here, enough to enable them,
without reporting particular facts, and still less names or papers
(names, indeed, they need not know), to say that they are satisfied
that such plans have been in agitation. Could you supply us
with anything that might tend to the same object ? It might be
very useful in the view of embarking the nation heartily in the
support of a war if unavoidable " (Auckland MSS. xxxv. 381).

The " Reflections," it should be remembered, were published in the autumn of 1790, in the halcyon days of the Revolution, while the doings of the French Constituent Assembly were still a matter for rejoicing on the part of the majority of enlightened people in England, while France, busy with domestic reform, desired above all peace with her neighbours and freedom from interference.[1] In those days and continuously from then, Burke preached his crusade against France, in constant communication with the continental Powers who plotted to crush her liberties. " Diffuse terror ! " Burke wrote to the emigrant princes, and he had the satisfaction of seeing his injunctions obeyed. Abroad, he conspired ; at home, he incited. He was the never-failing inspiration of British Tories in their denunciation of the Revolution ; in and out of Parliament, in and out of season, he persisted in his magnificent abuse, and in his determination to assist a war with France, " to keep the French infection from this country, their principles from our minds, and

[1] The first National Assembly of France had an early opportunity of proving its pacific foreign policy in the Nootka Sound crisis between England and Spain in the autumn of 1790. Spain, under the terms of her alliance with France, claimed the latter's help in the event of war with England, which seemed possible. The French Assembly unhesitatingly contradicted the views of the King's ministers on this point, and issued a declaration that no war could be entered upon without its assent, at the same time repudiating all wars of conquest or aggression, and, as an earnest of its pacific intentions, it ordered the chained figures of conquered nations which ornamented the statue of Louis XIV to be removed.

their daggers from our hearts." "It is with an armed doctrine that we are at war," he wrote in 1796. He had himself helped to arm it, and it was the weight of his armour which prolonged the war.

Peace might have been secured in 1793. The professed objects of the war were then attained. Dumourier had been driven out of Holland, the Austrian Netherlands were secure. The French made offers of peace, but we rejected them as providing " no indemnity for the past or security for the future." Obligations to Austria for her assistance in saving Holland were mentioned as one reason for continuing the war, and England was then pledged, by the repeated statements of her ministers and by the complexity of her continental engagements, to a war for the extermination of Jacobin principles, the likelihood of the success of which seemed as far off as the stars. Again it was said, as it had been said so often during the American War, that if the cause of the enemy were to be successful, there would be an end of all civilized government, and the monarchy of England would be trodden in the dust. In vain Fox pointed out the hopelessness of such an undertaking, and its inconsistency with the war's professed aims. " A war to exterminate principles," he declared, " will mean a war to all eternity." " The human mind is roused by oppression." " Impotent are the men who think that opinions can be so encountered. There are some things which are more successfully vanquished by neglect." He reminded Pitt of Lord

Chatham's oath, that he would die in the last breach before he granted the independence of America, and that one of the first of his own political acts had been to sign the independence which his father had so abhorred.

In the autumn of 1795 the King's Speech to Parliament indicated for the first time, though vaguely, a willingness to consider the possibility of peace. The idea, until then declared so ignominious, improper, and degrading, of considering the Government of France as one with which any peaceful relations could possibly be maintained, was giving way, under the pressure of social distress, financial difficulties, unrest in Ireland, and recognition of the unreliability of our allies, to a longing throughout the country to have done with war. Curious inconsistencies even then marked the position and the language of ministers. Though Robespierre had fallen, there was very little reason in Pitt's main argument that the existing Government of France was more capable than any of its predecessors had been of maintaining foreign relations. At least, its predecessors had not been less capable. Prussia's example might have reassured us on this point. Prussia, who during 1794 had only been induced to keep her army in the field by the subsidy we gave her, and even then had done her best to avoid any fighting, had concluded peace with France six months previously, and was at that moment reaping the fruits of her faith in France's stability of government in being able to devote her attention entirely to Poland. From the beginning, France had been capable of maintaining foreign relations ; there had been no complaints from neutrals that the Brissot Government, or even Robespierre himself, had failed in their contracted engagements.[1]

Moreover, the reason from which ministers appeared to derive such comfort, that France was then in the greatest possible distress, and her Government possibly on the point of collapsing altogether, seemed hardly the best encouragement that security in respect to treaties could at last be counted upon.

Finally, we had let slip the opportunity of making peace to Holland's advantage and security, and had chosen to wait until she was again lost, though we had her colonies in our safe keeping,[2] and the aggrandizement of France was certainly less defeated than it had ever been.[3]

---

[1] We ourselves were not particularly scrupulous towards neutrals. We threatened Switzerland, Genoa, and Tuscany, because they had not abandoned a neutrality which we considered criminal. This was our behaviour to small States who had not been aggressed upon, nor were inclined to be aggressive, in a war which we had entered upon in order to protect the small and weak, and towards which we had declared that we should have remained neutral if it had not been for specific aggressions.

[2] Including the Cape of Good Hope and Ceylon, which were described in the confidential sketch of the proposed terms framed by the Ministry for submission to the King as " the most valuable of our conquests " (Dropmore Papers, iii. 239–42). We gave back the Cape to Holland in the Peace of 1802, but kept Ceylon.

[3] In neither of these respects—i.e. the freedom of Holland and the check to French aggrandizement—were the circumstances of the Peace of 1802 any better. By the Peace of Amiens France retained possession of Holland, Belgium, the left bank of the Rhine, Italy, and Switzerland. From the commercial point of

Such were the circumstances which called forth Burke's " Letters on a Regicide Peace," the last furious outpouring of his unquenchable hatred of the Revolution, which had already done so much to multiply its consequences.

" What, you would treat with regicides and assassins ! " cried Burke, flinging his dying strength into passionate denouncement of his countrymen's disposition to relax hostility against an enemy he himself would have defied to eternity. " This false reptile prudence," " these oglings and glances of tenderness," he said, ill became a proud nation. " We are not at the end of the struggle, nor near it. Let us not deceive ourselves, we are at the beginnings of great troubles."

It is very magnificent, almost Promethean, this inexorable determination of Burke's to be on no terms whatever with those of whose incurable iniquity he was persuaded, and to delude no one that he minimized the dangers and the length of the struggle, a determination growing stronger and more embittered with the increasing evidence of the insuperableness of the undertaking.

Burke's influence at this period, however, could not prevent negotiations, which took place belatedly, and failed. The failure arose out of a specific question, the restoration of the Austrian Netherlands, concerning which we were pledged to Austria, and does not add to, or detract from, the

view as well, the terms of 1802 were most unfavourable to us, as they left the prohibitive tariff which France had imposed against us on the Continent still in force. England's actual indemnities were Ceylon and Trinidad.

arguments advanced by Burke. These reach
beyond particular circumstances, beyond the immediate context of the war with revolutionary France,
as also do the answers which Charles James Fox
repeatedly made to them.

" Shall we treat with regicides and assassins? "
said Fox, investing the question with all the scorn
and horror of Burke's gestures. " What ! Treat
with men whose hands are yet reeking with the
blood of their sovereign ! Yes, assuredly we should
treat with them. With them, be whom they may,
we ought and ultimately must treat who have the
Government in their hands." " Where the power
essentially resides, thither we ought to go for
peace." " If the contrary were true, if we treat with
France only when she has a Government of which
we approve, good God ! " said Fox, " we shall
fight eternally." Were we, he asked, to stake
the wealth, the commerce, and the Constitution of
Great Britain on the probability of compelling the
French to renounce certain opinions for which it
had already been seen they were prepared to contend to the last extremity? France should suffer
the penalty of her own injustice. Why were the
people of England to suffer because the people
of France were unjust? " We would never treat
with the present Government of France " ! Was
it likely that the French Government would ever
negotiate for its own destruction? Or was evidence of a more peaceful demeanour to be obtained
in war? Could it be said to the enemy, " Until
you shall in war behave in a peaceable manner, we
will not treat with you "? " That two nations

should be set on to beat one another into friendship is too abominable," said Fox, "even for the
fiction of romance, but for a statesman to lay it
down as a system upon which he means to act
is monstrous." "It is in the nature of war to
widen, not to approximate."

"What! you would treat with tyrants? Why
not?" answered Fox. "Do we not daily treat
with tyrants? I would have treated with Robespierre, not because I did not think his Government the most detestable tyranny that ever existed
but because England has nothing to do with his
tyranny." The question was, he said, not what
degree of abhorrence ought to be felt of French
cruelty but what line of conduct ought to be pursued consistent with British policy, which had
hitherto accepted the theory that every independent
nation had a right to regulate its own government.
To deny this, Fox said, was to act upon a set of
most unprincipled delicacies, to which no heed at
all was paid when committing the national honour
and safety into the hands of allies. From ministerial indifference to the conduct of the allies
towards Poland, Fox said that he could only infer
this maxim : "Make peace with no man of whose
good conduct you are not satisfied, but make an
alliance with any man no matter how profligate
or faithless he may be."

"Whatever our detestation of the guilt of foreign
nations may be, we are not called upon to play
the part of avengers." "Hatred of vice is no
just cause of war between nations," he argued.
"If it were, good God! with which of those

9

Powers with whom we are now combined should we be at peace? Security? Are we never to have peace because that peace may be insecure? A state of peace immediately after a war of such violence must in some respect be a state of insecurity. We must be satisfied with the best security we can get : it will, at any rate, be not less secure than a state of war. To go on fighting as a speculation, that perchance we may gain a better peace some time hence—what can this do but add to the sum of human horrors? Is war a state of probation? Is peace a rash system? Is it dangerous for nations to live in amity? "

These extracts from, and abridgments of, Fox's speeches [1] show the other side of the war against the " armed doctrine " to that to which politicians and writers of to-day think fit to call attention. They show it as no " other side " has ever again been shown, for these " bones of a giant," as Lord Erskine called the speeches, edited as they were from rough notes, communicate the wisdom and much of the brilliancy of expression of one of the greatest of English orators and most honest of English statesmen.

Burke and Fox were once companions. The French war parted them. It is due to their memory, as well as to the memory of their times, that, when the spirit of the one is recalled, that of the other should not be forgotten.

[1] "Speeches of C. J. Fox." Edited by Wright. With a Preface by Lord Erskine. 1815.

WAR
AND THE
WOMAN'S
MOVEMENT

WAR AND THE WOMAN'S MOVEMENT

By A. MAUDE ROYDEN

AMONG the influences making for international understanding, the Woman's Movement has been reckoned by its supporters to be one of the strongest. This was before the war. The latest International Congress held by the Suffrage Alliance, in Budapest, 1913, had not only impressed all who followed its deliberations by its numbers, enthusiasm, and unanimity, but also by the intensity of feeling with which many of the most brilliant speakers sought to enlist the women of the world in *la guerre contre la guerre*.

It is true that the passion for peace—the horror of war—was expressed by continental and rarely by British or American delegates. This fact only served to remind the latter of the grim reality of the war problem in countries like Germany and France, and perhaps to create the feeling that our own interest in it might not always be so academic as to most of us it persisted in seeming. Certainly one of the inspiring motives of the Congress was the hope that a movement, international, like that represented by the Suffrage Alliance, which brought together in a common hope the women

of America, Asia,[1] and Europe, must tend to create
the good feeling which in its turn makes for peace.
Delegates were reminded that women know the
suffering of war without its glory ; that its horror
and its sacrifices come to them shorn of the
glamour with which men have surrounded it ; that
it destroys all they hold dear and all they have
created ; that they have nothing to gain by it and
everything to lose. A speech made in this sense
by the most eloquent woman there—Mme Marie
Vérone—brought her audience to its feet in a frenzy
of enthusiasm, clapping, waving, and cheering,
while those fortunate enough to be on the plat-
form precipitated themselves upon the orator with
cries of enthusiasm, and kissed her on both cheeks
with an *abandon* somewhat surprising to the more
stolid British delegates. It was evident that there
was no doubt in the minds of these enthusiasts as
to the attitude of the Woman's Movement towards
war.

Conviction was deepened by the great chapter
on " Women and War " appearing in Olive
Schreiner's " Woman and Labour." Expressing
with a noble idealism the right attitude of women
towards war, Olive Schreiner gave to an emotion
its philosophy. Women, she said, were not only
the worst sufferers from war: they were by nature
the guardians of life. Conservers of the race,
mothers of its children, war must be to them

[1] No Asiatic delegates were actually present at Budapest, but
a Chinese Suffrage Society applied for affiliation, and was
admitted. The Chinese women sent a banner to the Congress
inscribed, " All of one mind, helping each other."

the worst of all catastrophes. As a sculptor would cast into the breach any stone rather than that which he had wrought into a statue, so women, when the gulf opens between the nations, would cast in anything rather than the men they have made. "No woman who is a woman," writes Mrs. Schreiner, "says of a human body, 'It is nothing.'" This phrase, like the whole chapter in which it appears, became a classic of the Woman's Movement. It was believed to express the true, the inevitable attitude of women as a sex, whether in or outside the progressive ranks. It was assumed to be so "natural" to them, that to put power into their hands was to forge a weapon against war. It was not denied that they might feel that war might in some cases still be a national duty ; but it was believed with conviction that women, from their very nature, would approach the question with an unspeakable reluctance, that war would appear to them in all its naked horror, shorn of glory, that they would be free from the "war fever" to which men so easily fall victims.

In support of this view, it is to be borne in mind that women's internationalism has on the whole broken down less conspicuously than men's, two international congresses having been held since the war began, and both representing women. It is probably also true that among working people the desire for peace is still stronger among the women than the men. On the other hand, the belief that women are innately more pacific than men has been severely shaken, if not altogether destroyed. It is now very evident that they *can* be as virulently militarist, as blindly partisan, not as ' the soldier, for in him such qualities are generally absent, but as the male non-combatant, for whom the same cannot always be said. Among women, as among men, there are extremists for war and for peace ; pacifists and militarists ; women who are as passionately convinced as Bernhardi that war is a good thing, women who accept it as a terrible necessity, women who repudiate it altogether. All these views they share with men. There appears to be no cleavage of opinion along sex lines. Nor perhaps should we have expected it. History shows no war averted by the influence of women ; none against which women, as women, have worked, or organized, or offered more than here and there a sporadic protest. Queens have been no more reluctant than kings to look on the dead bodies of men and say, " It is nothing." The fact that war brings to women personally no glory, but only suffering, is empty of significance ; they are well accustomed to vicarious glory and well accustomed to suffering. The appeal to their loyalty comes with irresistible force. " We cannot fight," they say ; " let us at least be willing to suffer."

Not what is noble only, but what is ignoble in women, is enlisted easily in the service of war. The importance of fear as a factor in war-making cannot be overlooked, and can hardly be over-estimated. Any politician can play on panic when he wishes to stampede a people into war. The

fear of being attacked enables him to blind them,
and makes them an easy tool for a war which is
really one of aggression. And in the creation
of panic a sex trained to timidity is hardly likely
to play a restraining part. Personal courage is
the one quality held indispensable in a man: it
has not been extraordinarily admired in women,
and since fear is the mother of cruelty, it should
not surprise any of us if those who have never
been expected to be brave should sometimes outdo
the men in vindictiveness. That so many women
remain untainted by fear should rather give us
hope. Nevertheless, it is reasonable to remember
that so long as fear plays a part in the making
of wars, women are hardly likely as a sex to
be more uncompromising in their desire for peace
than men.

It should, therefore, have surprised no one
(though, in fact, it surprised many of us) that
women throughout Europe have accepted war as
an inevitable evil, or even, in the earnestness of
their loyalty, as a spiritual good. Nor does their
attitude towards war in general, or this war in
particular, prove those wrong who have believed
that the Woman's Movement is one of the great
influences making for peace. It is true that its
effect will not be so direct or so obvious as had
been supposed. The mistake has been rather about
the nature of its influence than about its ultimate
effect. Women may, when they have the power,
no more " vote against war " than men ; it remains
a fact that every woman who is working for the
advance of the Woman's Movement is, however

martial she is herself, however profoundly she may mistake the meaning and the foundation of her work, working against militarism. She is for ever asserting a principle of which war is a perpetual denial. One principle must, in the end, destroy the other.

The Woman's Movement in all its aspects, but especially, of course, in its political one, is an assertion of moral force as the supreme governing force in the world. If its adherents are wrong, and it is physical force which is " the ultimate appeal," then the militarist is right, and the physically weaker sex, like the little and weak nation, has no claim that may not be set aside. The weak have no rights in a world governed by brute force ; they have only privileges, which may be granted, revoked, or withheld. It has been the fundamental principle of the Woman's Movement that it claims rights and duties, but never privileges. By what right, however, do those who are inferior in physical force ask to share, equally with their superiors, in government, if government rests on physical force? Such a claim could not be entertained. And women, recognizing this, have rightly based their demand on the great principle that government rests upon consent, and that the use of physical force is not " the ultimate appeal," but a confession of failure.

Argument has raged round this vital question, and in consequence the women's position—and that of the opposition to it—has been again and again defined. The " physical force argument " has been put forward with great effect and with an enthu-

siasm no Bernhardi could exceed by notable Anti-
Suffragists.[1] In their writings and speeches the
conviction that women could have no right to self-
government while they lacked physical strength to
enforce it has been expounded in terms which
almost grotesquely resemble the expositions of
" Prussianism " and the treatment of " little
nations " which have burned themselves with
such horror into our memories to-day. " The
State is Power," says Treitschke ; " there is
something laughable in the idea of a small State."
What power? Certainly not moral power, for
there may be a greater moral power in a little
State than a big one. But physical power, in
which the big State must be superior. " There is
something laughable " in the idea that a little State,
a people wanting in sheer force of numbers and
arms, should dream of independence, of freedom,
of developing along its own lines its own civilization. " Something laughable " ! There is also
something obscene in such laughter—something
unimaginably brutal. The same brutality (though
we had not learned to call it " Prussianism ") found
something laughable in the idea that women, who
are inferior to men in muscle, should claim as
" rights " what could (if allowed at all) never be
more than privileges in a world ruled by brute
force. Certainly if the world is so ruled the claim
does become laughable. Herein lay the weakness
of the militant movement, which appealed to a
principle which the whole Woman's Movement was

[1] See especially " The Physical Force Argument against
Woman's Suffrage," by A. McCallum Scott.

concerned to deny. But even here, regardless of logic—or perhaps conscious of a deeper logic than their policy suggested—the women who resorted to violence frequently argued that they did so only to prove the utter failure of violence used against themselves. Nor can any misunderstanding on the part of Suffragists of their own position destroy the fact that it rests upon a principle which militarism denies. The strife between the two is internecine. Militarism and the Woman's Movement cannot exist together. Take a militarist religion like that of Islam, and you see women reduced to the lowest level of degradation ; a militarist legal code like the Code Napoléon, and you have women without human rights and only sex functions—breeders of potential soldiers merely ; a militarist civilization like that of Prussia, and again women without rights, almost without privileges, women lagging behind their sisters in other civilizations otherwise near akin to them. "You do not know what it is like to be a woman," said a prominent German Suffragist, " in a country which has built its whole existence on a successful war."

As militarism waxes or wanes so, in inverse ratio, does the Woman's Movement. In Russia —a race essentially pacific, whatever criticisms may be brought against its Government—women hold a much higher position than in Germany. In France, a country once "militarist" to the core, but now no longer so, the Code Napoléon remains, the legacy of the arch-militarist, Napoleon ; but the higher level of civilization reached to-day reflects itself in the improved actual (as distinct from the legal) position of French women. In Norway and Sweden, countries so earnest in their desire for peace that their division into two kingdoms under separate sovereigns was actually effected (though with some soreness and jealousy) without a war, women have in one case actually achieved political freedom and in the other are upon the verge of it. In America women hold a high position, and are constantly improving it. In Great Britain both the friends and the foes of their movement illustrate the same truth.

There has been—perhaps still is—a section of public opinion in this country which believes that the British Empire is held together by the sword. It has even been stated that India is " held at the point of the bayonet." The fact that for a long time our mighty Empire was seldom without its " little wars " somewhere along its vast frontiers gave colour to a belief which otherwise seems actually grotesque. And it is significant that the opponents of Women's Suffrage were largely drawn from the ranks of this school of imperialist thought. Their argument was developed along two lines : one, that women could take no part in the business of holding the Empire by the sword, the other that they could not " think imperially." The latter argument was frequently put forward by women so obviously capable of performing the duty whose possibility (to other women?) they earnestly denied, as to remove its sting and its effect. The former was the real line of defence, and as long as this Jingo school of imperialism remains so long inevitably must there be an irreconcilable party of opposition to the Woman's Movement in this country. Its wane and the rising of a nobler conception of Empire has coincided with the gathering strength and power of that movement. Both spring from the same root—the belief that government, whether of a nation or an Empire, must rest upon consent, or confess its failure ; that moral force is not nobler only but stronger than coercion ; that an Empire " held at the point of the bayonet " must fall to pieces at the first shock of danger, while one in which there is freedom for the least as well as the greatest of its members stands " whole as the marble, founded as the rock." We do not imagine to-day that New Zealand, with its population of two or three millions, has less right to the free development of its own type of civilization than we with our fifty millions. We do not call that right a " privilege," or find " something laughable in the idea of a small State." We do not assume that there are no rights where there is not power to enforce them. On the contrary, we know that such rights can never be violated except at fearful cost to the violator. Not only does the act of injustice brutalize his conscience, but it vindicates again the principle which must at last react against him. Nations have assumed the right to act solely in their own immediate interests so far as they have the power to do so ; but no nation can always be the strongest, and the time will come when another stronger arises, or many strong ones find their common interest against the violator, and

then the old insistence that might is right destroys
what it had set up.

In a deeper sense also the strong stand to lose
by a violation of the rights of the weak. Mr.
Lloyd George, in one of the noblest passages of
a great speech at the beginning of the war, spoke
of the debt owed by humanity to the little nations,
who brought to its lips some of the " choicest
wines." And we would add that even those little
nations who have no specially glorious history, no
radiant names, have yet enriched the civilization
of the world by their difference and variety of
type. To crush out all those who have the right
to exist but not the power to enforce that right
is to commend to one's own lips, not the " choice
wine " of humanity but

the bitter dregs of woe
Which ever from the oppressed to the oppressor flow.

The spirit which disregards this danger and
despises this loss to civilization is " militarism " ;
and those who assert that rights remain rights
even when they cannot be enforced, and that the
moral law violated by physical violence vindicates
itself in the end by the destruction of the destroyer,
are fighting against militarism, whether they desire
it or not. The Woman's Movement is based on
belief in the moral law. It is concerned to assert
the supremacy of moral force, and it can show that
wherever the rights of the weak are set aside there
enters into the State an element of bitterness and
hostility on the one side, of brutality and moral

stupidity on the other, which lowers its standard of strength and effectiveness as well as of moral nobility.

It is true that although the principles of militarism and feminism are fundamentally opposed many people do not know it, and—since we are not a peculiarly logical race—many Englishmen and women who are genuinely shocked at Prussianism as expounded by Bernhardi and applied to Belgium, have themselves expatiated eloquently in the same vein when the question was of classes or sexes instead of nations. There are militarists who believe themselves feminist, and feminists who are undoubtedly militarist. And, after all, since we are most of us perfectly aware that "logic is not a science but a dodge," we must beware of dismissing a paradox merely because it involves an *apparent* contradiction. When, however, the contradiction is real—when the opposition between two principles is fundamental—the human mind cannot for ever hold them both. One must drive out and destroy the other. Those feminists who had most closely thought out their position had already grasped the issue. When war broke out, and ordinary political activities were necessarily suspended, it seemed to them as inevitable that they should take up the task of combating the real enemy of women (and of civilization)—militarism—as it was that they should take their share in the relief of the physical miseries and material burdens of war. There was no question of opposition to the war itself within the great Suffrage organizations, since the vast majority of their members believed that war had been forced upon us and was, on our part, a battle against a militarist ideal. But there was a deep consciousness that the spirit of militarism is very hardly separated from the fact of war, and that this spirit is immovably opposed to the feminism which rests its whole claim on the supremacy of spiritual force. War, indeed, has its spiritual passion ; but the fact that this must find its expression in the crudest forms of violence tends to exalt the latter at the expense of the former. Women can do no greater service to the world than to increase the healthy scepticism of violence as a method of imposing ideals which the history of religious persecution has already created.

War may claim for itself the power to destroy and to clear the ground. It can never construct or create. It is not the means by which ideals are imposed. There is ultimately no way of combating a wrong idea but the setting forth of a right one. Whether they are right who believe that moral force is " the ultimate appeal " against which coercion is vain and violence merely a counsel of despair, or they who see in physical force the real basis of government, let time show. One thing at least is certain—that as the Woman's Movement embodies the one creed and " militarism " the other, so these two must be in eternal opposition. The victory of one is the defeat of the other. Women, whatever other claim may be made for them, are not equal to men in their capacity to use force or their willingness to believe in it. For them, therefore, to ask for equal rights with men in a world governed by such force is frivolous. Their claim would not be granted, and if granted would not be valid. Like the negro vote in America, it would be a cheat and a delusion. But if moral power be the true basis of human relationship, then the Woman's Movement is on a sure foundation and moves to its inevitable triumph. Its victory will be an element in the making of permanent peace, not because women are less liable to " war fever " than men, or more reluctant to pay the great price of war, but because their claim and its fulfilment involves the assertion of that which war perpetually denies.

THE
ORGANIZATION
OF PEACE

THE ORGANIZATION OF PEACE

By H. N. BRAILSFORD

Two hundred years ago the Abbé de Saint-Pierre was completing the publication of his " Plan of Perpetual Peace." With cynical punctuality the European Powers have celebrated each centenary of its appearance with a universal war. Not all our humiliation before this spectacle can blind us to the fact that these centuries have brought with them some developments favourable to an enduring peace. The rise of national States has set limits to the arbitrary extension of kingdoms by conquest, marriage, or inheritance. The growth of self-government has introduced the factor of the popular will as a barrier against artificial wars of intrigue. The development of political morals has reached a point at which none of the greater civilized peoples will to-day avow that it is engaged, or ever could engage, in a wantonly aggressive war. This last safeguard seems of little practical worth, as we listen to the arguments which even Socialists in opposite camps have put forward to prove that their motive in supporting this war was purely defensive. Yet to doubt the sincerity of the conviction which has animated every European army in this war, that it is fighting for national security, would be to despair of the future of mankind. Fallible and liable to sophistication as this general instinct against aggression is, it is the only foundation on which the reformer can build. On the last Sunday of peace we saw the German Socialists crowding to mass meetings to protest against the thought of war. A week later the same men in uniform were marching dutifully towards the Belgian frontier. They had in the interval acquired the conviction that the Fatherland was threatened. No scheme, no treaty, no mechanism, if peoples desired war, would ever prevent it. But mechanism may have a function, if it can so illuminate the attitude of parties to a dispute that peoples will not again err so tragically in judging the question whether their rulers are embarking on aggression. Our difficulty to-day is not merely to prevent aggression : it is first of all to detect it.

If our problem be to utilize this general condemnation of aggression in the abstract, our first step must be to discover some test by which aggression can be distinguished from defence. The crude test " Which side first declared war? " is not decisive. Few neutrals held that the Boers were the aggressors in 1899, though Mr. Kruger, for strategic reasons, was the first to declare war. The alternative test, on which German public opinion laid stress in this war, " Which side first ordered a general mobilization? " is not more conclusive. The belligerent who seems the more correct in the last stages of a crisis may none the less have been on the whole the more exacting in his diplomacy, and may have manœuvred his opponent into mobilization or a declaration of war.

More puzzling still is the discrepancy between the legal and moral conceptions of aggression. The legal standpoint regards that Power as the aggressor who attempts by force to make a change in the *status quo*. The *status quo* may, none the less, be morally indefensible. The Balkan States were legally the aggressors in their attack on Turkey in 1912, but the Turkish oppression of their kinsmen was itself a prior aggression. In its efforts to conserve peace, diplomacy has always tended, more or less consciously, to set before itself as its objective the maintenance of the *status quo*. The presumption was always against the Power which attempted to disturb the existing order. The existing order might have come about as the result of successful aggression in the past ; it might consecrate countless wrongs in the present ; but a certain sanctity none the less belonged to it, because it was embodied in treaties and recognized by Governments. The conception is not wholly without value, and it has been, like all conservative institutions, the salutary check to rash ambitions and reckless disturbance. It breaks down whenever a nation, oppressed by some genuine grievance, or inspired by some proper ambition, feels that it has at last the means of making its claim good by force. Its prime error is that it allows no place in the common life of nations for radical changes and large reconstructions. A satisfied Power, which sees all its kinsmen free within its own frontiers, which enjoys full liberty to trade, and has in a vast Empire all the scope for economic expansion and emigration which it can fairly desire, is always apt to conceive of peace in this conservative sense. Desiring no great changes in its own interest, it regards nations which do experience some imperative need of change as disturbers of the world's peace. The consequence of a timid diplomatic tradition, reinforced by the conservative interests of the satisfied Powers, is that peace has always seemed to be a condition of passivity and rest. The structure of Europe has been, with rare exceptions, so inelastic, so dangerously rigid, that no considerable change could take place without war or the imminent risk of war. Through decades or generations of peace nations grow, their trade expands, their problems multiply ; grievances accumulate, and unsatisfied ambitions develop an explosive violence. With the outbreak of war frontiers become fluid, and there is no change which victorious force cannot propose to itself. A whole library of books and pamphlets written since this war began outlines the vast series of changes which public opinion in the belligerent countries desires, and in vain desired before the war. If we were to eliminate from these programmes all that is extravagant and egoistic, there would remain salutary changes enough to transform the map of Europe and rewrite its public law. After fear, it is the pressure of this need of changes, unrealizable during peace, which forces war. Leibnitz said of the Abbé de Saint-Pierre's scheme, based as it was on an eternal *status quo*, that " perpetual peace " is a motto appropriate only to a graveyard. The fundamental vice in the structure of Europe has been that it has never known how to provide for large changes without war. We must beware, then, of seeking our criterion of aggression in a disposition to disturb the established order or upset the *status quo*. If large organic changes must always be postponed till " the next war," there can be no enduring peace. If we dwell too simply on the single purpose of preventing war, we may drift insensibly into a conservative organization which would stereotype abuses, delay salutary changes, and repress the most vital political and economic movements of our time. Our problem must be, not merely to prevent war, but to secure such an organization of Europe that large international changes may be compassed without war.

We have seen that there exists at present no ready-made standard which a democracy, informed by goodwill and possessed of some measure of power, can apply to distinguish an aggressive from a defensive war. Where, then, shall we find our criterion? It must lie in some appeal from the interested judgment of each people in its own cause to the verdict of some calmer corporate conscience, which will reach its conclusions under the guidance of a view of the common good. What its organ in each case should be—a tribunal, a mediator, or a common council of Europe—we need not at once discuss. The principle is not new, but it is far from having secured general assent. No nation or Government entirely disavows it, but few have yet given it their firm adherence. It underlies the eagerness, as marked on the German as on the Allied side in this war, to secure a favourable verdict from neutrals on their policy.   Every nation, including Germany, has in the past submitted grave disputes of a justiciable kind to the arbitration of an international court, and an advance by which all Governments would bind themselves to submit all disputes of this limited class to arbitration is not only conceivable but probable.   It is not such disputes, however, which commonly lead to war, and if they should do so, it would only be because they were seized upon as a pretext which concealed a much larger issue. No civilized State can afford to make war over the interpretation of the wording of a treaty, over a boundary dispute, or over questions of financial compensation arising out of wrongs done to their citizens abroad.   It is when a dispute transcends the scope of any question which can be submitted to a merely legal settlement that the risk of war arises, and a reluctance to accept or even to invite the formal opinion of some neutral body makes itself felt.   Recent experience is not encouraging. France submitted her claim to a privileged position in Morocco to a conference of all the Powers, but it cannot be said that she was scrupulous in observing its decisions.   Austria, with German backing, refused a conference to sanction her annexation of Bosnia.   Sir Edward Grey's proposal to submit the dispute between Austria and Serbia to the mediation of the four disinterested Powers was decisively rejected by the German Chancellor, and his rejection was conveyed in a trenchant form which seemed to imply a dislike of the principle underlying any such procedure. He would hear nothing of an " Areopagus " ; he would not summon his ally before a " court " ; he seemed to imply that it was beneath the dignity of a Great Power to allow the interference of others, even in its external affairs. This attitude is no new pose in diplomacy. It has been the common form of conservative statesmen, and we may find an echo of it in Canning's motto : " Every nation for itself, and God for us all." There was something to be said for this attitude in Canning's day. Europe remained through the greater part of the nineteenth century a collection of isolated sovereign States. Alliances were never permanent, and were rarely contracted save for some limited purpose or for a single war. Our own generation has witnessed the growth of the permanent alliance, a combination formed not merely for war but for the normal conduct of diplomacy, and for trade and finance as well as for war. " Each for himself " is a motto which no longer answers to the facts. Europe consists no longer of six Great Powers and some minor States, but of two great groups which tend to draw the minor States within their orbit. These groups persist in peace no less than in war, and it is easier to conceive of their amalgamation into a single loosely knit league than to imagine their dissolution into their elements. In the old days it was possible for two Governments engaged in a dispute to reject the meddling of other Governments as an impertinence. At the worst they would fight out their quarrel between themselves ; the conflagration could be " localized," and with reasonable prudence no one else need fear that his house would blaze. To-day the links are so close that almost any war involving a Great Power must be a universal war. The affectation which resents the interference in a dispute of Powers which must presently be forced by their engagements to take part in it, is an unreasoning arrogance. The alternative to Areopagus is Armageddon, and the Powers which will not meet in council are only too likely to meet upon the battlefield.

The new organization of the impartial conscience, whatever it is, must be permanent. It is possible that the attempt to secure the reference of the Bosnian and Serbian questions to a conference failed precisely because the machinery of such a conference had to be improvised. It was possible for a conservative Austrian or German statesman to argue that some loss of prestige might be involved in going before a conference, because this procedure is still exceptional, and because if he yielded on this occasion, he had no security that other Powers would do so when his own interests might require this method of settlement. There may be wide differences of opinion as to what form the standing council should take, and with what powers it should be invested. It is probably hopeless to expect at first an agreement in advance from all the Powers to abide by its decisions. The tradition of the sovereign State, bound by no laws but its own supreme self-interest, will die hard. The minimum at which we must aim, and without which nothing appreciable will have been won, is an agreement that every Power will consent to submit every threatening dispute to the study of a standing council, and to refrain from war until its recommendations have been issued. If to this were added the much less controversial agreement to refer the narrower category of justiciable disputes to the arbitration of an international legal tribunal, we should have gained the objective criterion which we are seeking. The Power which broke its agreement to have recourse to the standing council, or declared war before its recommendations had been issued, would stand condemned before its own people, its allies, and the world of neutrals. By a single test which would admit of no sophistication or special pleading, it would be convicted of wanton and lawless aggression. If it should happen that the council issued recommendations which one party to the dispute refused to accept, the case would be only a little less clear. The party which rejected its recommendations would be guilty of flagrant aggression if it then went to war to enforce its own point of view. The other party, if it went to war to give effect to demands which had the sanction of the council, would be entitled to the sympathy, if not to the active support, of the rest of the world. No one could say that it was in the wrong in pressing its demands ; whether it did right to press a just demand to the point of war, would depend on the gravity and urgency of its grievance, and the extent of the risk which its action might involve to other peoples.

The Europe in which we live is no longer a collection of isolated States ; it is a community knit by permanent alliances. A scheme of this kind must adapt itself to the existing structure of the Continent. On the eve of this war, Sir Edward Grey put forward what he described as a " utopian " proposal (White Paper No. 101). It was that each of the two allied groups should guarantee the other against the aggression of any or all of its members. A verbal disavowal of aggressive intentions would add little to the real guarantees of peace, even if it were enshrined in such a formula as was proposed in Lord Haldane's negotiations of 1912. This scheme for arbitration or conciliation gives us for the first time an objective test of aggression, and enables us by means of it to limit the scope of alliances to an honestly defensive purpose. Nearly all alliances are in form defensive only, but the vagueness of the distinction between aggression and defence renders this restriction of small value in practice. If this scheme were honestly adopted, it would involve the insertion in all treaties of alliance (if the system of alliances survives) of a clause which would free the contracting parties from any obligation to give aid to a partner who had refused to submit his case to arbitration or to the Council of Conciliation, or gone to war before the period of delay expired. To this condition it seems to me indispensable to add a clause cancelling the obligations of the alliance if either ally should become involved in hostilities by reason of his own refusal to accept the recommendations of the Council. The advantages gained by this plan are, therefore, (1) the gain of a period of delay in which public opinion, if it be pacific, can act ; (2) the registry in each dispute of an impartial recommendation for its settlement ; (3) the setting up of a clear objective standard, by which the citizens of a would-be belligerent Power might judge whether its Government were acting aggressively ; (4) the isolation of an aggressor, through the abandonment of his cause by his habitual allies. This last provision, as Europe is constituted to-day, would generally be decisive. It would mean that the aggressor would fight alone, while his victim could invoke the aid of allies. The agreement for delay, arbitration, and conciliation would be still more impressive if it further required all the signatory Powers to concert military and other measures against any Power which broke it.[1] It is not, however, proposed in this minimum scheme that any Power should bind itself in advance to accept or enforce the recommendations of the Council of Conciliation, or that it should sign away its abstract right to go to war if the process of conciliation has failed to bring about a settlement which it can accept.

The real pivot of this moderate plan for the prevention of war is the period of delay, usually defined as one year from the date of the submission

---

[1] In describing the moderate minimum I have followed broadly a scheme of which a persuasive account will be found in Mr. Lowes Dickinson's "After the War" (Fifield, 6d).

of a dispute to the council. No proposal which promises so much can be free from difficulties. The first obvious difficulty, for which provision must be made, is that some disputes arise from continuous injuries, so serious that they must be suspended while they are examined by a Court of Arbitration or a Council of Conciliation. No Power will wait a year for justice, if the offender continues to repeat his aggression or completes a wrong whose beginning was already an offence. The Court or Council must be always in being to issue a preliminary injunction, in urgent cases, before the question of principle is debated.

Another difficulty turns on the change which might take place in the relative military preparedness of the disputants during the year of delay. An aggressive Power is commonly a well-armed Power. If it meditates a brutal use of force, it will usually have accumulated armaments and provided itself with allies. To ask it to wait for a year is in effect to deprive it of a great part of this advantage. Let us cherish no illusions about the easy realization of a scheme which to men of good will seems so eminently reasonable. The year of delay would frustrate the calculations by which militarist cliques and general staffs time the outbreak of disputes for the moment when their own strength is at its maximum and that of their adversary at its minimum. This handicap on military preparedness will be accepted only when every Power has consciously resolved to debar itself for the future from the speculative use of such advantages. Moderate as the scheme is, it exacts a complete breach with the tradition of militarism. The proposal originated in the Anglo-American Treaty, and it would work smoothly across the Atlantic between two cousinly Powers which have full confidence in each other. In a European dispute, we must prepare for some embarrassing possibilities. A year would enable us to improvise an army, while our opponent would increase his fleet. The unready Power would set to work to accumulate munitions and to build strategic railways. If it went still further, and started mobilization, the strain would become intense. American advocates of the scheme have laid stress on the psychological advantages of delay. Nerves would be calmed ; the press would grow weary of a protracted excitement, and warlike passions would be extinguished in boredom. Would that happen on the Continent? Each day might bring its tale of the enemy's new gun, his giant airship, his invincible submarine, his hastily laid railways, his intrigues to gain a Balkan ally, and finally his stealthy mobilization. If, moreover, a legal state of war were declared (or in our country the Defence of the Realm Act put in force), there would be an end of free discussion and a stifling of public opinion. It is clear that the amount and kind of preparation which is allowable must be carefully defined in advance. To allow preparation would indirectly discourage heavy armaments in time of peace, and give an advantage to the unready, which is often, but not always, the more innocent and pacific Power. It would, however, place a heavy strain on the forbearance

11

of the better prepared Power, usually the Power which is the more likely to defy the scheme, or even to reject it in advance. I confess that I do not myself clearly see the solution of this dilemma. The wiser course would be, I think, to forbid any new preparations in excess of those already publicly sanctioned by the Budgets of the Powers involved, and to forbid either mobilization or the declaration of a state of war. These prohibitions, if they did not extend to the whole year, might at least cover nine months of it. In calling attention to this difficulty, I am far from suggesting that it should deter us. We start from the belief that until war actually breaks out the party of good will is normally the stronger. It fails partly because it never has time, partly because it rarely knows the facts, and partly because it becomes unpopular by attempting to argue that the enemy is not wholly in the wrong. Give it a simple case to urge, with " Keep your Treaty and wait a year " for its single watchword, and it must carry the day, unless the conscience of its country be wholly perverted or crushed.

To attempt a full discussion of the composition and procedure of the Council of Conciliation lies beyond the scope of this essay. These questions have been studied in minute detail by the Fabian Society, and its draft treaty for the establishment of a Council is full of good suggestions.[1] It is important to decide whether we aim at a European League or at a world-organization. There is

[1] See the Supplements to the *New Statesman* of July 10 and 17, 1915.

much to be said for the former ideal.   Europe
makes some approach to a common level of culture and political development.   It is a unity which
has a meaning for the imagination and the
emotions.   To go far beyond the real ties of
fraternity would be to make the League a formal
and mechanical organization.   No political unity will
ever be real which is not felt.   On the other hand,
in spite of the Monroe doctrine, we should all wish
to include the United States, and Japan is already
within our political system.   Most of the Great
Powers are, moreover, World-Powers, and the
friction between them arises often from extra-
European questions.   The Fabian Society's solution
of a World-Council, which might on certain questions divide into European and American chambers,
sitting separately, is ingenious and promising.
With it we may agree that the ancient fiction of
the equality of sovereign States must be abandoned.
The Council must be free to reach its decisions by a
majority vote, and the voting power of each State
must bear some relation to its real importance
in the world.   This detail leads us rapidly to a
thorny question of principle.   Is our Council to
be a diplomatic congress, composed of delegates
instructed by their Governments?

On our answer to this question depends our
ability to move away in this advance from
the traditional methods of diplomacy.   Those
methods were well adapted to their end, the
furtherance of the restricted interests of the
national State.   The success of our Council
would depend, however, on its ability to face each

question on its merits, and to keep in view the general good of the European Commonweal. If a dispute arises, say between Serbia and Bulgaria, we shall get no objective decision on its merits if the Russian and Austrian members of the Council view it primarily from the standpoint of Russian and Austrian interests, while the British, French, and German members feel bound to adopt the standpoint of their Allies. We desire the nearest approach to abstract justice, consistent with the general interests of the whole European community. The diplomatic tradition starts from the maxim, *Do ut des.* A Council composed of diplomatists would hardly differ from such gatherings as the Congress of Berlin, where everything went by barter. There would be no voting on merits, but rather an elaborate traffic in votes. Incorruptible himself, the typical diplomatist has been trained to think primarily of his own country's interest. In the end, before " justice " could be done to Serbia and Bulgaria, their patrons and friends would be offering " compensations " all round to secure support, and the question at stake would turn on the solution of a dozen outstanding issues unconnected with the Balkans. It is because statesmen know so well by what methods congresses are " worked " that they are reluctant to submit to their decisions. A Council of diplomatists would fall at once into fixed groups, and a solution would be reached by the process of seducing some representative of a group from his habitual allegiance by the offer of considerations valuable to his country. An austere and

high-principled Foreign Minister might set his face
against such methods and impress his views upon
his delegate, but if it were suspected that even
one or two votes in a close contest had been
turned by these practices, the recommendations
of the Council would have lost all moral value.
We may fairly invite a Power to submit its case
to an impartial Council, capable of deciding a
question on its merits. But no Power would
submit to be outvoted if it knew that the majority
against it had been composed of rival Powers,
each of which voted with its eyes fixed on its
own irrelevant ends.

The middle course of nominating men of individual distinction for a fixed term, who would
not be expected to take their instructions from
their respective Foreign Ministers, meets this
difficulty in some measure. Everything would turn
on the character of individuals. Some would be
firm, impartial, and independent, and would resist
improper pressure. Others would be weak and
pliable. Some Governments would send the ideal
man, and trust him. Others would instinctively
choose a man on whom they could rely to obey
instructions, and the process of barter would go
on behind his back. A Council so comprised would
be a mixed body, but the average result of its
work might be good. These nominees, however,
would occupy a delicate position, and it could
never be certainly said that their decision represented either the official view of Governments or
the free view of peoples. It would be at the best
the verdict of a very distinguished and venerable

body of typical individuals. That might serve our purpose admirably, if we aim chiefly at a committee of conciliation for disputes. It would not serve so well if we wish our Council to act also as a legislative body. A Legislature must represent either governments or peoples.

There is another possible solution, bolder and more difficult than either of the others. It is that we should attempt to create a Council which will represent, not the Governments but the peoples of Europe—an assembly which would be, in fact, a European Parliament. It might be elected on a basis of population, by the popular chamber of each national Parliament, on a system of proportional representation. If the British representation were fixed, for example, at ten members, these ten would reflect the divisions of opinion prevailing in the House of Commons. It would consist always of some Liberals, some Conservatives, and at least one Socialist and one Irish Nationalist. On some questions it might be unanimous, but it would not always speak or vote as a united national delegation. In a Council so composed, natural groupings, based on opinion, would be formed across the lines of racial and national cleavage. The Council would not inevitably fall into a German-Austrian group struggling against a Franco-Russo-British group for the balancing votes of the smaller States. While a section, perhaps the majority, of each national group might follow on most questions a purely national policy, there would be, as time went on, some formation of true international parties.   The Socialists would be the first to come together.   A Progressive party would inevitably be formed for the extension and development of the federal idea.   A Conservative party would be created as naturally to uphold the sovereign rights of the national State.   Another natural line of division would be that of the Free Trade and Open Door tendency against the Protectionist and monopolist tendency.   Even if we suppose that the powers of the Council would at first be very limited, that its work would be watched with intense jealousy by the official custodians of national sovereignty, and that it could do little more than draft proposals and recommendations, which the sovereign national Governments would sometimes consider and often ignore, there would grow from the public debates of such a Council a real sense that Europe is a united society with problems, interests, and opinions which bind us all across our frontiers.   The true solution of international strife is not to kill it by the boredom of a dull and secret procedure.   It is, on the contrary, to elevate it to an open, honourable, and profoundly interesting discussion of opinions. Instead of dreading international " disputes " as mere curses and dangers, we must learn to regard them as we think of our differences in domestic politics, as the very springs of movement and change, the proof that we are alive and are adapting ourselves to our environment.

An elected Council would offer the natural solution of the main difficulty which confronts any advance towards international organization.   So

long as congresses and councils represent only
so many solid, impenetrable, isolated national
States, so long as they reach their decisions by
bargain and barter behind the scenes, no Power
will bow naturally or easily to their decisions, and
certainly no Power will bind itself in advance to
accept them.   We must go behind " Powers "—
the very word suggests nothing but parks of
artillery, squadrons of battleships, and massed
legions—to the populations which are capable of
thought on other than nationalist lines.   If a vote
against Great Britain meant merely that Germany
and Austria had " squared " the Scandinavian delegates and " compensated " the Balkan members,
so as to create a factitious coalition against us,
we might refuse to obey it, and rightly so.   But if
it meant that our advanced policy had been for
the moment negatived by the caution of a mixed
majority—a French Conservative voting with a
German Clerical and a Russian Slavophil—should
we feel the same sense of humiliation and injustice?
If it meant that our conservatism on some issue
had been overborne by the united Socialist vote,
backed by French Radicals and the advanced parties
of Norway and Holland, would we bow to the
majority much more reluctantly than our Conservatives do when a Liberal majority is returned at
home?

Another consideration tends to favour the
creation of an elected Council.   It is that problems
of peace and war tend to hinge ever less on
" disputes " between isolated Powers, and ever
more on larger questions of world policy—colonial

trade, the Open Door, the free use of straits and ports, the " freedom of the seas," and the immense issue whether backward but potentially wealthy regions are to be developed economically by the system of partition, monopoly, and concessions, or by a regulated international partnership, or by free competition. These are matters which call rather for a decision of principle than for the process of conciliation appropriate to narrower " disputes." We want for these purposes a standing Legislature, which can amend its own work from time to time, deal with details as they arise, and appoint its standing commissions to act administratively. The chief of its standing commissions would be the Council of Conciliation, which might sit in private, to handle the delicate business of adjusting disputes between single Powers. Others might take over each department of legislation and administration as it became ripe for international control, until as the decades and generations passed, a loosely knit consultative Council might evolve into a federal Parliament. If this proposal be too bold a starting-point, we might urge that while Governments set up some Council of delegates or nominees more in keeping with the present tradition of inter-State intercourse, to serve as the responsible and authoritative organ of a nascent European Commonweal, there should also be formed, beside it, and even below it, an elected consultative chamber, free to debate in public, to suggest new policies and urgent changes, and to send up its recommendations to the supreme Council and the national Governments. It is not probable that Diplomatists will ever so far depart from the traditions of their craft as to propose the creation of an elected Council. It will come into being when Parliaments themselves take the initiative. No mechanism will ever give us perpetual peace. We shall have peace when Europe has developed an international mind. The prime value of an elected Council would be that it would give to this mind a corporate personality and an articulate voice.

We must in all candour inquire, before we close this brief study, how far the moderate minimum of a Council of Conciliation, fortified only by an agreement to allow a year's delay before the outbreak of war, would answer the requirement we have laid down. Would it give such a presumption that great and necessary changes may be effected without war, that Governments would refrain from the competitive armaments and the partisan alliances which are to-day the means of moulding the world to the will of the strong? Formally it offers no such security, for it is not proposed that Governments should bind themselves in advance to accept the recommendations of the Council, nor that neutrals should constitute themselves its executive arm. The consequences of these limitations would be serious. In the first place, the temptation to arm, though it might be weakened, would not be removed. Secondly, it would be difficult to argue that alliances had lost their purpose, and there would still tend to be an inevitable grouping of Powers with a grievance or an ambition against those which opposed its redress or satisfaction.

The understanding that alliances became invalid if the agreement for a delay to allow of arbitration or conciliation were broken would, indeed, tend to make them less absolute and less menacing. But in some degree we should still live in the atmosphere of the armed peace and the balance of power. In the third place, the Council, moving warily amid these dangers, and conscious that it possessed no means of overcoming the self-will of the disputants, would be chary of making recommendations which might be disregarded. Its recommendations would at first be timid ; they would bear an undesirable relation to the balance of military power, and would fall far below the requirements of ideal justice. Would it dare to touch the really dangerous grievances, the wrongs which at a perceptible rate accumulate the explosives of war? It could not, for example, safely propose for many years after this war to upset any of the arrangements of the final settlement favourable to the victors, however inequitable they might be. It would probably shrink from recommending a Great Power to carry out any difficult act of reparation or surrender, though it would be bound for its own credit to suggest some solution which would ease the tension. If it dared not, for example, propose a surrender of territory, it might at least suggest the concession of autonomy to its inhabitants. These limitations are not an objection to the scheme, but they are a warning to us that the power of any mechanism to bring us within reach of objective justice, and to prepare large changes without recourse to arms, will grow only as we develop the international mind and equip it with the organs of an international Government.[1]

By what means can this evolution be hastened? It will, no doubt, be proposed that some League of Peace be formed with a definite military basis, which may back the claims of justice by an ever-ready force. Just in so far as such a league is partial, it must fail in its purpose. The Powers which do not enter it will combine against it, and they will have the sympathy and support of such minor States as dread the power of its members. A partial league which proposed to use force to back its ideals would soon reproduce the old divisions of Europe in a new form, and when it talked of enforcing peace and justice it would seem to those outside it that a façade of hypocrisy had been erected to mask the old fortress of the balance of power. The proverbial question would arise, *Quis custodiet ipsos custodes?* A, B, C, and D form such a coalition, while E and F remain outside it. The day comes—for all of us may err—when D contemplates or perpetrates a wrong against some weaker State. Will A, B, and C then proceed to coerce D? D, in such an emergency, would instantly ally himself with E and F, and the choice for A, B, and C would either be to renew the general war, or to abandon the moral

[1] The general case for an advance to a federal organization and for a scheme of conciliation, stiffened by an authority which can impose decisions, is stated with compelling force in Mr. J. A. Hobson's "Towards International Government" (George Allen & Unwin, 2s. 6d.).

basis of their league. It would be wiser to leave
our rudimentary organ of justice without organized
military support than to create behind it a league
which involved the exclusion of any of the greater
European Powers.

The true answer to these foreboding riddles
is that every fresh advance in international
organization, and especially the creation of
economic ties, will help to make good the inevitable
defects in any rudimentary mechanism of conciliation. The scheme of conciliation must not be
allowed to stand for long as the sole link between
rival and isolated Powers. If the league which
has accepted this principle could be evolved into
a commonwealth, which conferred great and evident
benefits upon its members, a new motive would
be forged which might be used to secure obedi-
ence for its decisions. By force we shall never
constitute a true league, and any voluntary association of nations must admit the right to secede.
If membership conferred certain measurable
advantages, secession from it would be difficult,
and the league, as it grew strong, would be able
to lay down the principle that any failure to
observe the decisions of its council involved secession and the forfeiture of its privileges.[1] What
these privileges might be, it is easy to suggest
in outline. The ideal arrangement would be a
league which translated its political unity into a
system of Free Trade confined to its own members,

---

[1] I have attempted a sketch of a league with such an economic
basis in the new chapters of the third edition of " The War
of Steel and Gold " (Bell, 2s.).

while it maintained an appreciable but not necessarily prohibitive tariff against the imports of
outsiders.   If any disloyalty to its political constitution automatically entailed secession, and
exposed the seceder to the higher tariff, its
decisions would have a powerful sanction behind
them.   This ideal may be remote, but some approach to it may be possible.   If the league
could not at first construct a true Customs
Union, insuring to its members full Free
Trade within all its territories, we might begin
with an agreement to accord to all its members the
benefit of a " most-favoured-nation " clause ; this
at least would put an end to tariff wars within
it.   We might go on to arrange for the abolition
of differential tariffs in non-self-governing colonies ;
a reform which would go far to remove any motive
to the forcible acquisition of colonies, for if I
may freely trade with my neighbour's colony, I
shall not desire to conquer it.   We might next
arrange that members of the league should
accord to each other such freedom of access to
their money markets as allies commonly concede
to each other, and perhaps a guaranteed proportional share for the capital of members in big international undertakings in Africa, Turkey, and China.
Only by some arrangement of this kind shall
we be able to turn the flank of the capitalistic
Imperialism which fosters Militarism for its own
economic ends.

It has often been proposed that a trade boycott
or complete non-intercourse should take the place
of war as a means of putting pressure on an

aggressive Power. Such methods, effective in themselves, could with difficulty be organized or enforced by States which in normal times were bound by no close economic ties. To apply them would require an effort so violent, and would seem to the offender an outrage so extreme, that they might rather provoke war than prevent it. A league accustomed in times of peace to differentiate in its tariffs between members and non-members, and to make economic advantage the token of its political unity, might use this method smoothly yet with deadly effect. It is an axiom that the closer our international organization becomes, the more firmly and the more boldly will it venture to use its authority.[1]

It would be idle to attempt to sketch a detailed programme for the future, or to speculate on the pace of our advance. We do not know in what mood Europe will look around it and face its problems when the havoc of this war is ended. It may be so wearied, so anæmic, so riven by hatreds, so robbed of hope or energy, that any forward step, however timid, will demand our utmost efforts, and our strength will be spent rather

[1] These proposals must be carefully distinguished from the suggestion which is now being put forward in all the allied countries, that the Allies should, after this war, combine to exclude or penalize German trade. That suggestion is merely punitive and vindictive, or else it is a sentimental disguise for a crude trading egoism. Apart from economic objections, no plan would so surely perpetuate hate. The suggestion in these pages is that the economic weapon should be used impartially, not to satisfy resentment for the past, but to ensure peace for the future.

in resisting a desperate recoil into barbarism and reaction. It is also conceivable that our experiences may beget a revolutionary temper, which will first in certain countries break down the internal obstacles to change, and then sweep forward with a new impetus towards a bold international reconstruction and a sharp breach with the intolerable past. At the worst we shall have before us at least a ten years' truce of exhaustion in which to raise our barrier against the next outbreak of folly. The first test of the resolve of a new Europe for enduring peace will be the ability of its peoples to impose on their Governments a preliminary agreement to accord a year's delay for conciliation before they fight. The Government which concedes so much will have turned its back upon the past and broken the spell of centuries dominated by force. Without this indispensable foundation we shall build in vain. On it a new Europe, inspired by so great an act of faith, might with confidence erect by gradual stages and logical extensions the firm structure of a federal league.

DEMOCRACY
AND
PUBLICITY IN
FOREIGN AFFAIRS

DEMOCRACY AND PUBLICITY IN FOREIGN AFFAIRS

By PHILIP SNOWDEN, M.P.

THE Great War will have been fought in vain if
it has not taught the working classes of Europe
the paramount necessity of publicity in foreign
affairs.   When the multi-coloured books contain-
ing such notes and dispatches as it has suited the
several Governments to give to the world have
been exhausted in the effort to apportion the responsibility for the war, the conviction must be
left upon the mind of every impartial person that
a system of diplomacy carried on in secret is an
anachronism in an age when democratic government is, in every country in Europe, acknowledged,
more or less, to be a sound principle for the control
of domestic politics.

Unless it can be shown that there is something
in the nature of foreign affairs which distinguishes
them so radically from domestic politics that the
accepted principles of national government are
quite inapplicable to the control of foreign policy,
then the present system of conducting foreign
affairs stands condemned.   But an examination
of the arguments advanced against the popular

control of foreign policy reveals the fact that they are precisely the same as those which have been invariably employed against every demand for the extension of political liberty and the enfranchisement of the people.

The case for the popular control of domestic policy can be stated in a simple but sufficient phrase. It is that every citizen of a State has a right to a voice in determining the extent of and the form in which the State shall interfere with his personal liberty. In these days the formula of democracy cannot be fully expressed in the old phrase, " Taxation without representation is tyranny." Every year the State interferes more and more with the life of the individual. It regulates his conditions of work, his business, his wages, his housing, his education, and disposes of an ever-increasing proportion of his personal property. Nobody publicly suggests nowadays that we should revert to the old political system under which the disposal and direction of the lives and liberties of the people was in the hands of a king or aristocracy. Because the acts of Government and Parliament affect the condition of the people it is an uncontroverted doctrine that the people should control the political affairs of the nation.

With the object-lesson of this war before the eyes of the nation the concern of the people in foreign affairs needs neither emphasis nor exposition. We see the lives of the people sacrificed by hundreds of thousands ; taxation is being imposed upon all classes to an extent which seems likely to be a heavy, if not intolerable, burden upon them ; we see, perhaps for our lifetime, the high hopes we had entertained of a great social reconstruction dissipated ; we see the wealth and energy which should have been devoted to dealing with the problems of child life, of education, of public health, of unemployment, of housing, and with all those industrial and social evils in our land, devoted to the destruction of life and treasure on a scale so vast that the imagination reels before the spectacle.   This surely is the concern of the masses of the people.

The war is the outcome of foreign policy. We are not concerned here to apportion the blame or the responsibility.   The war is the failure of diplomacy.   It may be the fault of German, or French, or Russian, or Austrian, or British diplomacy, or of all in some measure.   The system of secret diplomacy, the divorcement of democracy from the control of foreign affairs, is common to all European countries.   The war is indisputable proof that this system of diplomacy has failed to maintain peace.   It may, of course, be argued that any system of diplomacy or of the conduct of foreign affairs would not prevent war.   But the first answer to that assertion is that this system has failed, and that the result of that failure is a calamity so colossal that no other system of diplomacy could be more disastrous.

Two conclusions, therefore, must be accepted— namely, that the results of foreign policy are of the most serious concern to the people of every country, and that whether it be possible or not to devise some system of foreign policy and of the conduct of foreign affairs which will prevent or lessen the disastrous results of international policy with which we are now painfully familiar, the present method is a failure. The failure of the present system of diplomacy justifies us in not only considering, but in demanding, some change in the control of foreign affairs.

The conduct of foreign affairs, in all European countries, has, up to the present, been in the hands of a small body of diplomatists, rulers, and ministers. Neither Parliament nor the people know what is going on in the secret chambers of diplomacy. The nations are committed to the most serious obligations without their knowledge. The whole history of foreign affairs consists of policies adopted, treaties arranged, and wars undertaken without the previous knowledge of the people so vitally concerned. In 1911 we were on the brink of war with Germany over the Morocco question. If war had actually broken out, there were not at that time a hundred people in England who would have known what it was about. That crisis was due to the intrigues of a number of European Governments, pressed on by financial interests, to get free hands for the exploitation of certain parts of Northern Africa. Treaties were concluded, the terms of which were published ; but now we know that secret treaties were in existence which committed some of the signatories to an aggressive policy directly opposed to that to which they had openly pledged their word.

In 1912 the most important negotiations were

going on between this country and Germany, with
the object of improving the relations between the
two countries. Of these negotiations the British
Parliament and the British nation were kept in
ignorance, and only bit by bit, under the strongest
pressure, have the people been partially informed,
three years later, of what took place. When, in
March 1915, the Prime Minister was asked in the
House of Commons to put the country in possession of the full facts, he replied that " no public
advantage would be served by the publication of
the notes and dispatches " bearing on these vital
matters.

Such a method of conducting the foreign affairs
of a country is pure autocracy. It places the
destinies of a nation, the lives of the people, the
hopes and welfare of the democracy entirely at
the mercy of a small handful of persons. These
persons have the power to thwart all the aims of
the democracy in the sphere of domestic reform.
So long as such a power is in the hands of a few
persons democratic government is a mockery, and
the working classes are the playthings of rulers
and diplomatists. It is a monstrous thing that a
score of European diplomatists and rulers should
have the power to involve practically the whole
of Europe in a devastating war. By such a
system the nations of Europe are committed in
secret to tremendous responsibilities, and when this
system of diplomacy has brought the nations to
the verge of war, the people are induced to support
a war they have never wanted, and which they
have not expected, by appeals to their fear, their

party loyalty, and their national patriotism. Democratic government to be a reality must give to the
people control over such matters as treaty obligations with foreign countries, and Parliament must
be trusted with the final decision on such matters
and with the supreme question of peace or war.

The objections which are brought against the
demand for publicity in foreign affairs are precisely those which have done duty in every past
campaign against the extension of the political
franchise. It is said that the people do not understand foreign affairs ; that it is essential that such
matters must be conducted by men of special
knowledge and training. But experience of democratic control of home affairs has falsified all the
arguments and fears of the opponents of a popular
franchise. It is not, of course, maintained that
the democracy has risen to the full height of its
responsibilities and opportunities. It has made
many mistakes. It has often disappointed the
hopes of ardent reformers. But with all its fail-
ings and weaknesses democratic control of home
affairs has been a vast improvement, from the
point of view of national welfare, on the former
system of aristocratic government. The people
are slowly learning to understand and to use their
power, and every decade shows an advance in
the intelligence of the democratic vote.

We are justified in feeling a very considerable
amount of confidence that the system of democratic control which has for two generations been
the method for conducting our national affairs
would, if applied to the control of foreign affairs,

be equally satisfactory. If the extension of the franchise has not altogether changed the character of parliamentary representation, it has changed the atmosphere and outlook of Parliament. In regard to home affairs the rights and wrongs of democracy have become the main subject-matter of political contention and of legislative effort. The point of view of the working classes receives a consideration in Parliament now which was not possible when the landed aristocracy shared with the plutocracy the control of national affairs.

But as the control of foreign affairs is still in the hands of the same class which formerly monopolized all political power, the conduct of foreign affairs and the personnel of the Diplomatic Service have remained unchanged, and are still the preserve of the landed and privileged classes. The natural result of that system is that these affairs have not been conducted in the democratic interests, but in the interests of the same class whose evil control of home affairs gave rise to the great popular demands for the democratic control of domestic politics. The popular control of home affairs has brought the democratic outlook and sympathy into legislation ; and, in like manner, the popular control of foreign affairs would change the character of diplomacy. It would be recognized that the people were the controlling authority, and the administrators would naturally try to represent the people's point of view, instead of that of the financial and commercial interests. If it were known by our statesmen and diplomatists that the results of their diplo-

matic efforts were dependent for confirmation upon
the approval of the popular representatives, they
would strive to achieve such results as would be
likely to secure that approval.   In other words,
diplomacy, knowing that democracy was its master,
would endeavour to serve the interests of
democracy.

The question now arises for consideration
whether democratic control of foreign affairs would
insist upon a change, and whether it would
earnestly pursue a policy for the establishment
and maintenance of peaceful relations between
nations.   It would not be wise to dogmatize on
this topic, but it is permissible to submit evidence
which appears to give very strong support to the
belief that democratic control of foreign affairs
would tend towards the abolition of war.   The
breakdown of international socialism on the declaration of war was a grievous disappointment to those
who had built high hopes on the growing soli-
darity of the workers of the world.   But a calm
and fair consideration of all the circumstances
leaves one with little reason to feel despondent,
or to lose faith in internationalism.   Great movements grow slowly.   National prejudices are hard
to kill.   No great project ever succeeds at first.
It is only after many failures that triumph comes.
The international working-class movement was subjected to the greatest possible strain before it
had grown strong enough to bear the test.   But
the true facts are now becoming known, and one
may almost say that the matter which should cause
surprise is not the failure of international socialism

to prevent the war, but that in all the circumstances so much of the international spirit survived the terrible ordeal.

The workers in all countries hate war. That they support wars is no disproof of that statement. The amazing absence of anything of the nature of jingoism among the people of this country during this war, the universal desire to see an end of the war on such conditions as will ensure a permanent peace, show that the spirit of the democracy is not military but pacific. The democracy never support a war except for one or both of two reasons, namely, through fear, or to remove or avenge some real or alleged injustice. Since September 28, 1864, when the first International was formed in London, one of the primary objects of every international association of working men has been the promotion of international peace. The workers may be trusted to use their power and influence to prevent war because they know something of the terrible cost of war. They know they gain nothing by war. They realize that the common interests of the workers can be served only in the ways of peace. They know well that war and militarism are the instruments of capitalism and exploitation. They know that war is the greatest enemy of social progress, for it divides the working classes of the different countries and distracts their attention from the prosecution of what the continental workers call the " class struggle "—that is, the battle for the economic emancipation of the wage-workers.

The working classes object to war for other

reasons.   They know from experience that a time
of war is a period when the liberties they have
won in times of peace are easily filched away.
They know that the cost of war, wherever the
taxes may be directly laid, falls with the heaviest
weight upon them.   They know that bad trade
and hard times follow war, and that though individuals may gain from war, they as a class, and
the nation as a whole, are always the losers by it.
The working classes, by instinct and by knowledge,
are peaceful and opposed to war, and there is
every reason to believe that their influence on
foreign policy, so far as they might be able to
exercise it, would be all in the direction of promoting peace and the establishment of good relations between all nations.

Though the instincts of the people are towards
peace, it does not necessarily follow that, if there
were publicity in the conduct of foreign affairs,
there would be a greater likelihood of averting
wars.   But there are grounds for a reasonable
supposition that such a result would ensue.   Let
us bear in mind the fact that secrecy in diplomacy
has not prevented war.   On the contrary, the
policies which the rulers and diplomatists have
pursued in recent years have brought about the
Great War.   If we agree with the popular view
in this country that the Prussian militarists have
for years been preparing for this war, it is certain that the great Social-Democratic party in
Germany were ignorant of that movement.   On
the other hand, if the people of Great Britain had
been aware of the secret missions to foreign Courts

for the purpose of furthering a policy for the isolation of Germany, it is probable that public opinion in this country would not have approved such a policy. That this diplomatic policy was being pursued behind the backs of Parliament and the people was well known in the inner circles of the European Courts. After the mischief has been done, these truths have been permitted to come to the light. For instance, the Belgian Minister in London (Count de Lalaing), in a dispatch to his Government dated May 24, 1907, said : " It is plain that official England is quietly pursuing a policy opposed to Germany and aimed at her isolation, and that King Edward has not hesitated to use his personal influence in the service of this scheme."

Such a policy as that was bound to eventuate in war. If these facts had been known to Parliament five years ago this war would never have taken place, for the danger of the policy of attempting to isolate Germany would have been realized, and before matters had developed to the point of hostilities the public opinion of Great Britain and Germany would have interfered. Similarly the secret mission of Lord Haldane to Berlin in 1912 failed because of its secrecy. The disclosures made by the German Chancellor and by Sir Edward Grey show that the margin of difference between the proposals of the two Governments was so small that if there had been an earnest desire on both sides to come to an agreement the difference could easily have been bridged. The secret knowledge and the suspicion in the minds of both parties—the knowledge of the German Chancellor of the secret intrigues which for years had been going on between England, France, Russia, and Spain for the isolation of Germany, and the knowledge in Sir Edward Grey's mind of the secret understanding between this country and France—made it impossible for a satisfactory agreement to be reached. But if the final differences could have been submitted to the respective Parliaments, if the peoples of Germany and England, both anxious for friendly relations, could have been consulted, if in an atmosphere of peace these matters could have been discussed with full knowledge, it is as certain as day follows night that some basis would have been found for a friendly settlement.

But even if that had not happened, the advantage of publicity would have been immense. If the negotiations had failed, plainly because Germany was determined to accept no agreement which would not give her a free hand against France and Russia, then the public in all European countries would have known the real facts. If war was seen to be inevitable, our Government would have been in a far stronger position. Because they alone have been in possession of knowledge which they believed pointed to the possibility of war, they have been hampered in making the preparations for war. If it were the fact that the German fleet was being built to challenge the position of Great Britain and to attack this country, then the great increases in the Navy Vote of Great Britain during the last eight years might

have been justified. But because of the secrecy
of foreign policies the Government were unable
to justify their policy by a full statement of the
facts. Secret diplomacy makes the conditions for
war ; but where the control of finance is in the
hands of Parliament, it prevents the Government
from making the adequate preparations to support the commitments of that secret policy.

There is nothing in the nature of foreign affairs
which renders the public discussion of them un-
intelligible to the ordinary mind. If that were so,
why have the various Governments of the belligerent States taken such trouble to provide the
public with the notes and dispatches bearing oh
the war? The different Governments have based
their case on the evidence of these books. They
have appealed to the public to act as the jury
on this evidence. The people, it appears, are considered fit to form correct judgments after the
mischief is done, but unfit to be consulted before.
The matters with which foreign politics is concerned are no more difficult or subtle than many
questions of domestic policy. The Unionist Party
were at one time anxious that the electors of this
country should vote directly on the question of
Tariff Reform. That is one of the most abstruse
and difficult social, economic, and political questions, and the people who were to be asked by
their votes to decide this issue are the same people
who are not considered sufficiently enlightened to
decide whether British foreign policy shall be used
for, say, assisting to divide Europe into two rival
and hostile combinations, or for establishing a

concert of nations acknowledging a code of international law.

A great advantage which would come from publicity in foreign affairs would be in the parliamentary and public discussion which would arise. This public discussion would have a three times blessed result. It would have a restraining influence upon ministers and diplomats in the preliminary negotiations. The aloofness of foreign policy from parliamentary control and public discussion must have the effect of making foreign ministers and diplomatists rather contemptuous of Parliament and people. It must subject them to a constant temptation to do things which they would not do if they knew that their action would come before a committee of Parliament and be subjected to criticism. It would put an end to the secret intrigues of financiers and armament interests to direct foreign policy. The second great benefit which publicity would confer would be that the discussion of questions of foreign relations would help to clear away mutual misunderstandings between nations, which are so often due to the suspicion which secrecy always encourages. This discussion would bring the peoples of the different nations more closely together, because no such discussion of international relations could take place without making plain the common interests of the workers. The third great benefit which would result would be the gradual education of the democracy in foreign politics, the expansion of their horizon, and the development of the international spirit and outlook. When the democracies have the international spirit there will be no more wars.

We come now to the practical proposals for giving effect to our demand for publicity in foreign affairs. Reform will have to be carried out in three quarters. Some form of parliamentary control over foreign affairs will have to be established ; the staffs of the Foreign Office and the Diplomatic Corps will have to be changed, and the relation of the Foreign Secretary to Parliament will have to be altered. The control of Parliament over foreign policy is now merely nominal. It is true that an opportunity is provided by means of questions in the House of Commons for obtaining information. But the Foreign Secretary withholds information altogether, or gives just as much as he thinks desirable. Members of Parliament are restricted in their access to sources of information about foreign affairs, owing to the secrecy with which diplomacy is conducted. In the matter of questions dealing with home affairs the Member of Parliament is able, as a rule, to find out the actual facts for himself, and he then is in a position, by means of questions and supplementary questions, to meet the minister on fairly equal terms. But it is not so in regard to foreign affairs. A reference to the incident of the Japanese demands upon China in the spring of 1915 will illustrate the difficulty of a Member of Parliament eliciting the facts by means of questions in the House of Commons. That was a matter in which the honour and the interests of Great Britain were seriously involved. But questions to the Foreign Secretary failed to elicit any information as to the nature of the Japanese demands, or the progress of the negotiations, or of the attitude which our Foreign Office had taken up. The Foreign Secretary pleaded that a copy of the Japanese Note to China had been given to him by Japan in confidence, and the terms could not be divulged. What that meant was that, though Great Britain was by treaty bound to maintain the integrity of China, Parliament was not entitled to know anything about the action which our ally was taking to destroy that integrity.

In addition to the opportunity afforded by questions there is usually one day each session set apart for the discussion of foreign affairs. It is obviously impossible to adequately discuss such important and varied subjects in one sitting of the House of Commons. In normal times the House of Commons is so fully occupied with domestic legislation that it might be difficult to afford time for frequent discussions on foreign affairs. But there would be no difficulty in allotting at least as much time for that purpose as is given to the discussion of the Navy and Army Votes. It would be useless, however, to give more time unless Parliament were kept constantly more closely in touch with what was being done by the Foreign Office. To provide that closer acquaintance with foreign policy, the establishment of a Committee of Foreign Affairs is desirable. This committee should be composed of members drawn from all the political parties in the House of Commons. In time, service on this committee would provide a fair proportion of members who had acquired knowledge of this department, and who would be able to discuss these questions intelligently in the public debates in the House. Such a committee would not assume the responsibility which is now vested in the Foreign Secretary and the Cabinet. Its function would be to learn the facts and to act in an advisory capacity.

But no extension of parliamentary control over foreign affairs would be effective if the character of the Diplomatic Service and the constitution of the Foreign Office remained unchanged. The staffs of both the Diplomatic Corps and the Foreign Office are recruited in the most undemocratic way, and the personnel are quite out of touch with present-day movements. The nomination for the examination for a Foreign Office clerkship and for a post in the Diplomatic Service rests with the Foreign Secretary. The candidates are drawn wholly from one social rank. Candidates for the Diplomatic Service must give an assurance that they are provided with a private income of not less than £400 a year. If appointed, they must serve abroad for two years without salary. This condition ensures that the men shall belong to the well-to-do class, and, as a matter of fact, the utmost care is taken that only young men of high social rank are selected. Of twenty recent appointments one-half were peers or the sons of peers, and the remainder belonged to a social class scarcely less exalted. The Royal Commission on the Diplomatic Service which reported in 1914 said : " The effect of this condition [the required minimum private income of £400 a year] is to limit candidature to a narrow circle of society.   We have been furnished by the Civil Service Commissioners with the educational antecedents of the successful competitors for attachéships in the years 1908-13 inclusive.   No fewer than twenty-five out of thirty-seven came from Eton, while all but a very small fraction had been educated at one or other of the expensive public schools.   In only one case was any University other than Oxford or Cambridge represented.   No further evidence is required to show the limiting effect of the present regulations upon the class of candidates from which the Diplomatic Corps is recruited."

The two necessary qualifications for the Diplomatic Service are social rank and the qualities which will make a diplomat acceptable in the society of the Court to which he is accredited. Men of this sort can have no knowledge of the great democratic movements which are rising in all countries, and which are forcing on the attention of all Governments great social and economic questions.   These men have been reared in a world apart from the actualities of the present day.   They know nothing of the democratic or international spirit.   It was quite consistent to have such people to conduct foreign affairs when Parliament was controlled by the same class.   But to-day the Diplomatic Service and Foreign Office are anachronisms.   The reform needed is to throw open these Services to young men of all classes qualified by education and character.   Just as it is possible for the son of a poor man by the system of open competition, with the help of public scholarships, to obtain an important post in the home Civil Service, so it must be made possible for such to enter the Diplomatic Service and the Foreign Office, and to bring the democratic outlook and sympathy into the conduct of international affairs.

One oft-repeated objection to publicity in foreign affairs requires a word of comment. It is said that this reform is impossible unless all nations in diplomatic association simultaneously adopt the system, or that if this country alone did so it would be placed at a disadvantage in diplomacy. This is a reform which one country can adopt without waiting for a general agreement among the nations to do so. There can be no such secrecy as we desire to abolish unless all the parties conspire to preserve silence. The adoption of publicity in foreign affairs by England would bring to the light the dealings of other nations. The abolition of secrecy would no doubt place those at a disadvantage who desire to work in the dark because they fear the light and public opinion. If the aims of a nation's diplomacy are honest there is no reason why it should desire its movements to be covered by darkness.

But this objection appears to arise from a misunderstanding of what is meant by publicity in foreign affairs. There is no proposal that all the negotiations between the nations shall be conducted openly, and that every note and dispatch shall be made known to the world. That is obviously neither possible nor desirable. What is meant is that there shall be established some form of parliamentary control over foreign policy, that its general lines shall be directed by Parliament, and that no minister or Cabinet clique shall have the power to commit the word of honour of this country to any policy which has not been approved by Parliament, and which is not in accord with the general principles approved by the nation at a general election, and that the country shall know clearly how it stands in relation to other nations and what its obligations are. In other words, the abolition of secrecy in foreign affairs means that Parliament, which has now nominally the responsibility for foreign policy and war, shall be able to decide such matters with full knowledge, instead of, as in the past, being called upon to make a hurried decision on a momentous question, like the voting of supplies for war, in ignorance of the causes which have led to such a situation, or when the country has been irrevocably committed to war by the pledged word of its ministers.

The powers vested in the Senate of the United States, under the American Constitution, for the control of foreign policy afford an example of a method of securing some measure of publicity and democratic control. The sanction of the Senate is required for the ratification of a Treaty, and as Lord Bryce writes in his " American Commonwealth " (vol. i. p. 109) : " Yet different as the circumstances of England are, the day may come when in England the question of limiting the present wide discretion of the executive in foreign affairs will have to be dealt with. The

example of the American Senate may then be
cited, but there is this important difference between
the two countries, that in England Parliament
may dismiss ministers who have concluded a treaty
which it disapproves, whereas in the United States
a President, not being similarly removable by Congress, would be exempt from any control were
the Senate not associated with him in the making
of a treaty."

The qualification which Lord Bryce adds to his
statement that the example of America may be
cited in support of a change in the method of
conducting foreign relations by England has very
little force in the face of recent experience. Parliament may dismiss ministers who have been
carrying out a foreign policy it disapproves, but
the mischief cannot be undone, and the fact
that Parliament is only permitted to know what
ministers choose to tell makes it difficult or impossible for it to arrive at a firm conclusion,
and its uncertainty constitutes the security of the
ministers. The example of the American method
disposes of most of the theoretic objections to
more publicity in foreign affairs, such as that
foreign Powers will refuse to negotiate with a
country except through ministers who have plenary
powers, and that the country which has to submit
draft treaties to a parliamentary body will be
at a disadvantage in negotiation. The American
method would not be applicable to this country
in its precise form. Such a Second Chamber
as we have in England, or such as we are likely
to have, would not be a suitable body to exercise

control over foreign affairs. A Joint Committee of the two Chambers to consult and advise the minister, without relieving him of responsibility, would probably be a more useful body. To this body consideration of treaties might be referred, as they are to the American Senate, but the final confirmation of the treaty should rest with Parliament. The demand for publicity in foreign affairs is one phase of the age-long struggle for democratic liberty. It is a demand for the extension to the sphere of internationalism of the principle of popular government, which, whatever its weaknesses may be, is manifestly the only form of government possible with the advance of education and modern economic and social developments. The destinies of nations have been trusted to kings, nobles, and plutocrats, and they have each and all failed. We must now trust the people.

THE
DEMOCRATIC
PRINCIPLE
AND
INTERNATIONAL
RELATIONS

THE DEMOCRATIC PRINCIPLE AND INTERNATIONAL RELATIONS

By VERNON LEE

IT is not from any great belief in what is called
" constructive policy " that I want our reader to
think out some of the principles which should control the international relations of democratic
peoples. We do not know enough about the
materials and the forces which will make up the
Future for our ground plans and elevations to
have much importance, except in so far as our
wishes and efforts are themselves part of the stuff
that Future is made of. But in some measure, at
least, we know the Past, and even that prolonga-
tion of the Past called the Present ; and our
attitude to these, our desire to seek and avoid,
are themselves one of the unknown and incal-
culable Future's materials. What might we wish
if we stood in the Future, felt as the Future, in
short, were part of it? That is a useless question. But being ourselves part of the Future's
seed, it is not unimportant what we think about
our own Present, and especially our own Past.

This Present tends, or we wish it to tend,
towards a more and more democratic character.

Whatever may have been the line of least resistance towards the greater good for the greater number in ages past, that of our own day is evidently the democratic one. We have come to realize that in our more evolved societies such increase of present prosperity as will not hamper, but further the increase thereof in the future, is, or tends at least to be, more and more along the lines of individuals and collectivities being responsible for their own welfare, instead of being, as in the days of Divine Right and Church Authority, subjected to the responsibility of others. To believe in democracy means to believe that however great the drawbacks of freedom to think and choose, however many the delusions attendant thereon, yet such freedom is educative, and its very failures and pitfalls make those failures and pitfalls less frequent ; whereas even the most successful régimes of authority place the people who benefit thereby at the mercy of accidents themselves have not been educated to control. This being the case, we may, I think, start from the premiss that in asking ourselves, What are the principles by which the relations of Nations and States are best guided? we may ask, What are the principles of international relations which are most consonant with the general principles of democracy?

Foremost among these principles of democracy is hostility towards artificial privilege and monopoly. Our aversion to them is summed up under a sense of justice. We are offended, and more and more offended as we grow more ethically sensitive, by the sight of all avoidable inequality of chances. But besides this instinctive, and one might almost say this æsthetic, sense of fair play, there is beginning to accumulate in many of us a residue of experience telling us that artificial privileges and monopolies create confusion and deadlock ; bring about all manner of wasteful deviation and violent readjustment ; and jeopardize the power of human affairs to right themselves by mankind's instinctive shifting towards satisfaction and away from its reverse. The belief in freedom of thought, and the belief in freedom of trade, are not merely reasoned-out propositions which we can defend by argument ; they are also, to a considerable degree, accumulated residues of experience, habits of preference and action due to repeated, uncounted, and unnoticed experiences of analogous kind. We moderns believe in freedom in great measure intuitively, because we have adjusted ourselves to larger and larger doses thereof ; freedom, like justice, has become, apart from all analytic justification, something towards which we turn by what might be called our intellectual and emotional vital exchanges, as plants turn through their chemical and mechanical functions towards light and moisture.

Considering therefore democracy, not as a condition of affairs already existing, still less one having already existed, among men, but as a principle deducible from certain tendencies realizing themselves partially at various times, and more and more dominant in our own, we have to ask in what manner such democratic tendencies are affecting, and likely to affect, the relations of a Nation to other Nations, in other words, in what way democratic ideals make for Peace.

The democratic principle, a principle deduced from increasing practice and increasing that practice by its regulative application to it, may be roughly defined as that of consent as against compulsion ; agreement (with its correlate disagreement) as against obligatory authority ; and self-direction as against direction by others ; equality of judicial and civic rights being among the necessary guarantees of this threefold first principle.

In other words, we may say that the democratic attitude is one of greater and greater respect for freedom of choice, a greater and greater belief in the tendency of variety to produce by mutual selection and adjustment an ever richer and more supple social harmony. Let us see the application of this principle to politics. Within the bounds of one nation it goes against every kind of artificial privilege and monopoly, since these diminish freedom of choice and substitute compulsion for choice. In foreign relations it is evident that our democratic preference for consent as against compulsion diminishes and abolishes all supposed rights by conquest. Once recognize that only the consent of a people can decide their nationality and government, and you put an end to the possibility of countries or provinces being kept against their will, as Trent is being kept by Austria, for reasons having no present sanction in the inhabitants' wishes, and still more so of those countries or provinces being transferred, except from their free will, from one nation or régime to another. The imposition of a Russian régime on Finland, although Finland is not a Russian conquest, is against the democratic principle as much as the annexation of Alsace-Lorraine by Germany. The· secession of Norway from Sweden is perhaps the most hopeful practical recognition of this principle. In short, the democratic principle of consent *versus* compulsion, *ipso facto*, makes a country or province a portion of whatever country itself prefers.

To say, as Bismarck did to the dissident Alsatian deputies, that Alsace-Lorraine had not been annexed for its own convenience and safety, but for the convenience and safety of Germany, was to treat Alsace-Lorraine in an undemocratic spirit: as a chattel, a material possession existing only for its possessor ; and it was the way, of course, to place that possessor himself in the light of a mere material obstacle which those he thus treated as chattels would shake off whenever feasible. On the other hand, to say, as I have heard quite liberal-minded French people say of late, that Alsace-Lorraine should be reunited to France without a plebiscite or other consultation of its inhabitants' choice, because it is *stolen goods* and stolen goods can be taken back without more ado by their former proprietor, is to speak just as undemocratically as Bismarck spoke. It is, comically enough, to repeat verbatim the very excuse which Germany put forward in 1871 for that annexation. The very essence of the demo-

cratic principle is to consider men and women
as *wills* and not as *chattels* ; and the progress
of democracy, as it implies a constant diminution
of all possibility of exploiting individual men and
women against their choice, implies also that inhabitants do not belong to territory but territory
to inhabitants.   To transfer a province is therefore
as undemocratic as to sell a slave.   Thus, as
believers in the democratic principle, we are bound
to give our sympathy to the people of the province
of Trent when they declare their wish to be united
to the kingdom of Italy.   But we cannot respect
the plea of the Italian Government, or even of
the Italian nation, that the annexation of Trent
is requisite for the military safety of their country
or even for that equally self-regarding collective
advantage which is called the *satisfaction of their
ideal aspirations*.   Neither is there much to be
said, from the democratic point of view, in favour
of the motives for which we British have held
Ireland in a past which has not quite come to
an end, and shall continue to hold sundry other
places in the probable near future.   But since
hypocrisy is a tribute to the virtue (and one might
add, to the wisdom, the self-command, and clear-
sightedness) which the hypocrite has not got, so
also the progress of democratic morality and policy
is shown by the more and more frequent assumption either that a conquered country has called in
its conqueror (this was a frequent fiction in
Napoleon's time and also of the Holy Alliance
which conquered him), or that a country so
annexed is " protected " for its own good, is a

ward of its master, and will, once grown out of childhood, understand and bless the restrictions and the chastisements which may have chafed its foolish immature will.

I think it is clear from all the foregoing that the democratic principle absolutely rejects the notion of a military victory having "fruits." Such *fruits of victory* it calls by their real name of *loot*. No matter what sacrifices the victorious nation may have made or what risks it may have run, the democratic principle denies the right (which would sanction highway robbery and burglary) that the sacrifices and risks of Tom can be compensated by imposing sacrifices on Harry.

If human beings are to be treated as human beings with wills like our own (and this, like all morality, is wisdom, and like all wisdom, is morality), and not, as was avowedly the case throughout Antiquity and the Middle Ages, as chattels, slaves, or creatures you could keep or kill at convenience, then wars are absurd, useless, illegitimate, unless undertaken either in self-defence (including self-liberation) or in defence of some weaker party. And indeed the theoretic acceptance of this principle is shown in the present war, which each of the several belligerent Governments proclaims, and each of the belligerent peoples sincerely accepts, as a war either of self-defence (Austria defending herself against the vicarious encroachments of Russia in the Balkans, Germany against the threat of Russia and Russia's allies, France defending herself against Germany) or of defence of some smaller State, as Russia defending Serbia, and England, Belgium. That they can all be right in their assertions and beliefs is impossible, and may lead some sceptics to guess that they may all be mistaken in various or equal degrees. But the universal certainty of each belligerent about being a peaceful victim or chivalrous champion and his opponent an aggressive criminal, shows that though we are very far from acting upon democratic principles, as we are very far from practising Christianity, yet we have all of us explicitly or implicitly accepted those democratic principles as the only ones consonant with a good opinion of ourselves and a respectful attitude on the part of our neighbours.

In discussing these matters it is necessary to bear in mind that, as I set out with saying, we are at present dealing with democracy, not as any existing set of institutions but rather as a TENDENCY; and a tendency which is the only one in political and social relations at all likely to increase and become more universal and organized, despite all obstacles and set-backs. For the very essence of democracy being the admission of greater and greater numbers to self-government, and consequently the better and better equipment (by education, institutions, and also by habit) for self-government, it is evident that methods of conciliation and co-operation must be perpetually on the increase, and methods of compulsion and one-sided exploitation on the decline.

This democratic tendency towards adjustments more and more favourable to mutual advantage brings with it the greater and greater equivalence of what, looked at from two opposite sides, we are accustomed to oppose to one another under the names of *Expediency* and *Justice*. For in a régime of increasing self-government and increasing equality of chances and of the training these bring with them, it becomes more and more *expedient* for one individual or group to behave towards other individuals or groups in such a manner that these will feel that they are *justly* treated—i.e. treated with such reciprocity that they could obtain greater individual or group advantage only by *unjust* treatment of other individuals or groups, that is to say by methods which, given a régime of increasing equality, would jeopardize the safety of the aggressors and become, therefore, *inexpedient* to themselves.

In fact, democratic progress may be defined as that which gives to the moral precept " Do unto others as you would be done to " a constantly increasing sanction of expediency, and thereby an automatic application.

That such development must be slow and exposed to frequent set-backs (like that of this war) is merely another way of saying that in the present and future we have to pay the debts, and struggle with the difficulties, left by the Past, both in the way of habits of mind and of institutions. But although such progressive application of the democratic principle is slow and arduous (but constantly *less* slow and *less* arduous through the effect of its inherent tendency to conciliation and co-operative adjustment), yet such progressive application of the democratic principle is not in the least *chimerical* ; since it is, on the contrary, based less and less upon self-sacrifice and more and more upon the self-regarding wisdom of consulting the wishes of others to whom self-government and equality give the power of impeding the accomplishment of one's own.

Such higher expediency is, indeed, but an outcome of the practice of *barter* which is implicit in all democratic conceptions, that is to say, of *voluntary* giving what either party wants less for what either party wants more ; as opposed to *extortion* or *rapine*, by which one party obtains what it wants, but at the expense of the ill will of the other and a consequent loss to itself due to the necessity for coercion of the unwilling or vindictive loser.

Perhaps what I have called the Democratic Principle (which we are now considering because it is opposed to the militaristic principle and is a main factor of Peace)—perhaps what I have called the Democratic Principle is no other than the principle of progress in the political and social sphere. Or, rather, perhaps we might say that what justifies democratic tendencies in our eyes is the belief that, in our times at least, they make for an increasing betterment of human conditions. And mark ! not merely a betterment of the present at the expense of the future, or a betterment of the future at the expense of the present (both of those are alternately promised us by militarism and all kinds of tyranny), but a ratio between the two, by which, neither being unduly sacrificed to the other, the betterment of the future is, on the contrary, one of the results of a betterment of the present. Such a ratio between proximate and ultimate advantage implies economy of resources. A great deal of the world's progress in the Past has automatically compassed itself by the survival of especially gifted and resistant minorities, but at the cost of destroying, not only the present welfare (and often the bare existence !) of less gifted majorities, but depriving the world of whatever could have been got by the co-operation of those majorities for whatever they were worth. Indeed, progress such as we see it in the Past may be compared to the Past's imperfect methods of extracting the precious metals, by which a certain amount of them was of course secured in easily accessible grains or nuggets, but with the waste of enormous quantities of ore which required finer methods for its utilization. This is perhaps the reason why the history of Antiquity—and how much more the unrecorded history of primeval mankind as we guess it to have been !—strikes us as a series of wreckages, civilization after civilization rising out of a process of devastation and isolation, to be itself overwhelmed (layer on layer of burned towns and broken potsherds as excavations are showing us !) by the barbarism it had repressed or excluded or ignored ; wreckage out of which only a minimum of human acquisitions was saved and handed on by the wreckers. Those ancient civilizations, submerged one after another with such colossal waste of acquisitions and possibilities, were, we should bear in mind, carried on mainly on the

principle of conquest, compulsion, and ruthless exploitation of the adversary ; the vanquished being
either exterminated, driven into worse territories,
or made to toil for the victor either in actual
slavery or by means of tribute depriving them of
all but the barest subsistence, methods which
can be studied in more recent times in our dealings
with backward races. By these methods, as has
been pointed out by various social philosophers,
especially by J. M. Robertson, the potential pro-
ductivity of the world was enormously diminished ;
the victors often became, like the Romans, economically parasitic on the vanquished, who, on the
other hand, became less and less productive as
a result of their tyrannical exploitation.

Thus, adopting the phraseology of a recent
Austrian biological sociologist, Rudolf Goldscheid,
in his noble and suggestive " Menschen-Okonomie
und Höherentwicklung," one might say that the
waste of *Human Capital* under the slave-holding
and tribute-levying régimes of the Antique World
is parallel to the waste, the destruction of natural
resources, by the primitive husbandry which takes
everything out of the soil and puts nothing in,
which cuts down forests and never replants them,
and thus reduces countries, as so many of the
Mediterranean and Western Asiatic countries have
really been reduced, to barren rock and malarious
seaboard.

The manufacturing and trading communities of
the Middle Ages defrauded civilization to only a
lesser degree by envious legislation, which transferred the markets and industries of the vanquished

to the victors, and surrounded, for instance, medieval Siena and Florence with what had once been prosperous townships, and now became decaying, sometimes fever-stricken villages like Tiutinnano d'Arbia and Sovana, or even mere barely identifiable sites, as in the case of Semifonti, which the Florentines razed to the ground, scattering or absorbing its inhabitants. It was on the same plan of capturing alien trade that England ruined Ireland in much more recent times ; it is in the same spirit, and with the same amount of wisdom, that some of our contemporaries, even of those believing themselves to be democrats and reformers, are urging England to ruin, so far as is possible, whatever may remain of German industry and commerce at the end of this war.

I have given these instances lest the existence of certain forms of popular government should mislead us into imagining that the Democratic Principle of *choice* versus *compulsion* has been really recognized, let alone acted on, in the historic past. Democracy, in the most important sense we can attach to the word, is not a set of institutions. It is, I should again like to repeat, a tendency towards a particular mode of judging and acting, a tendency much more recent than we usually think, though of even vaster and more rapid growth. But the recognition of this comparative newness of such a democratic tendency, while obliging us to patience with its present imperfect realization, encourages us to wish and to strive for, as well as to expect, its less and less imperfect realization in times to come. And we thus obtain, not only

an aim for the future but, what I venture to consider as more important still, a criterion for the
present ; since, in proportion as mankind slips
out of its old notions of submission and dogma, it
becomes more obedient to the notion of consistency
and responsibility. The Democratic Principle that
men and women are not *things* but *wills*, and
the democratic régime of reciprocal concession and
mutual advantage, will therefore tend to realization no longer merely by such aggregate and
automatic action as we sum up under the name of
economic and *historic forces*, but also, and more
and more, by the conscious and deliberate choice
of every individual taken singly. Self-determination is one of the aspects of the Democratic
Principle. And self-determination will itself imply
that the Democratic Principle must supersede the
principle—if you can call it a principle !—of which
we see the crassest and most antiquated embodi-
ment in the present attempt of each and every
nation to establish security by violence and to
vindicate liberty by brute compulsion ; in other
words, to obtain the economic and moral bless-
ings of peace by means of the economic ruin and
the moral devastation of war.

UNWIN BROTHERS, LIMITED, THE GRESHAM PRESS, WOKING AND LONDON

Social Science Series

Cloth, 2s. 6d.   Double Volumes 3s. 6d.
*   Also in Limp Cloth   1s. net.
**   Paper Covers   1s.

SOCIAL SCIENCE SERIES—*(Continued)*

Edward Carpenter's Works

TOWARDS DEMOCRACY. Library Edition.
4s. 6d. net. Pocket Edition, 3s. 6d. net.

ENGLAND'S IDEAL. 12th Thousand. 2s. 6d.
and 1s. net.

CIVILIZATION : ITS CAUSE AND CURE.
Essays on Modern Science. 13th Thousand. 2s. 6d.
and 1s. net.

LOVE'S COMING OF AGE : On the Relations
of the Sexes. 12th Thousand. 3s. 6d. net.

ANGELS' WINGS. Essays on Art and Life.
Illustrated. 4s. 6d. net. Third Edition.

ADAM'S PEAK TO ELEPHANTA : Sketches
in Ceylon and India. New Edition. 4s. 6d.

A VISIT TO A GÑANI. Four Chapters
reprinted from Adam's Peak to Elephanta. With New
Preface, and 2 Photogravures. La. Cr. 8vo, ½clo., 1s. 6d. net.

IOLÄUS : An Anthology of Friendship. 2s. 6d.
net. New and Enlarged Edition.

CHANTS OF LABOUR : A Songbook for the
People, with frontispiece and cover by WALTER CRANE. 1s.
7th Thousand.

THE ART OF CREATION : Essays on the
Self and its Powers. 3s. 6d. net. Second Edition.

DAYS WITH WALT WHITMAN. 3s. 6d. net.

THE INTERMEDIATE SEX : A Study of
some Transitional Types of Men and Women. 3s. 6d.
net. Third Edition.

THE DRAMA OF LOVE AND DEATH :
A Story of Human Evolution and Transfiguration. 5s. net.
Second Edition.

INTERMEDIATE TYPES AMONG PRIMI-
TIVE FOLK : A Study in Social Evolution. 4s. 6d. net.

THE HEALING OF NATIONS. Crown
8vo. Cloth, 2s. 6d. net. Paper, 2s. net. Third Edition.

THE SIMPLIFICATION OF LIFE. From
the Writings of EDWARD CARPENTER. Crown 8vo.
New Edition. 2s. net.

The Pocket Edition of Ruskin

This Edition contains the Author's latest Additions, Notes and Indices.

Fcap. 8vo, Cloth Limp, 1s. 6d. *net* per Volume ⎱ Gilt Tops, Gilt Back,
Leather Limp, 2s. 6d. *net* per Volume ⎰ Autograph on Side.

Cloth Boxes to hold Six Volumes, 1s. each.

THE SEVEN LAMPS OF ARCHITECTURE. With 14 Illustrations.
[*70th Thousand*

MODERN PAINTERS. Vols. I., II., III., IV., V., and VI. (Index). With 315 Illustrations.

THE STONES OF VENICE. Vols. I., II., and III. With 173 Illustrations.
[*32nd Thousand*

LECTURES ON ARCHITECTURE AND PAINTING. With 23 Illustrations.
[*13th Thousand*

THE HARBOURS OF ENGLAND. With 14 Illustrations.
[*11th Thousand*

SESAME AND LILIES. Three Lectures and Long Preface.
[*129th Thousand*

THE CROWN OF WILD OLIVE. Essays on Work, Traffic, War, and the Future of England.
[*108th Thousand*

THE TWO PATHS. On Decoration and Manufacture. [*23rd Thousand*

TIME AND TIDE. On Laws of Work. [*60th Thousand*

A JOY FOR EVER. On the Political Economy of Art. [*62nd Thousand*

THE QUEEN OF THE AIR. A Study of Greek Myths.
[*48th Thousand*

THE ETHICS OF THE DUST. On the Elements of Crystallisation.
[*39th Thousand*

THE ELEMENTS OF DRAWING. With 50 Woodcuts.
[*27th Thousand*

THE EAGLE'S NEST. On the Relation of Natural Science to Art.
[*20th Thousand*

MUNERA PULVERIS. On the Elements of Political Economy.
[*20th Thousand*

UNTO THIS LAST. On the First Principles of Political Economy.
[*106th Thousand*

LECTURES ON ART. Delivered at Oxford in 1870. [*24th Thousand*

SELECTIONS FROM THE WRITINGS OF RUSKIN. Vols. I. & II. With Portraits.

THE STONES OF VENICE. Selections for Travellers. 2 Vols.
[*25th Thousand*

MORNINGS IN FLORENCE. Studies of Christian Art.
[*27th Thousand*

ST. MARK'S REST. History of Venice. [*16th Thousand*

FRONDES AGRESTES. Readings in " Modern Painters."
[*60th Thousand*

THE RUSKIN READER. [*9th Thousand*

The Pocket Edition of Ruskin (*continued*)

THE BIBLE REFERENCES IN THE WORKS OF RUSKIN.
[*7th Thousand*

ELEMENTS OF PERSPECTIVE. [*10th Edition*

THE POETRY OF ARCHITECTURE. With 29 Illustrations.

GIOTTO AND HIS WORKS IN PADUA. With 56 Illustrations.
[*7th Thousand*

ARATRA PENTELICI. On the Elements of Sculpture. With 22 Full-page Illustrations.
[*9th Thousand*

ARIADNE FLORENTINA. On Wood and Metal Engraving. With 16 Full-page Illustrations.
[*10th Thousand*

VAL D'ARNO. On Art of 13th Century in Pisa and Florence. With 13 Full-page Illustrations.
[*11th Thousand*

ON THE OLD ROAD. Miscellaneous Articles and Essays on Art and Literature, etc. In three vols.

FORS CLAVIGERA. With the Illustrations. Letters I. to XCVI. In four vols.

PRÆTERITA. Scenes and Thoughts in my Past Life. An Autobiography. With the Illustrations. In three vols. [*16th Thousand*

OUR FATHERS HAVE TOLD US. The Bible of Amiens. With 5 Illustrations.
[*11th Thousand*

THE ART AND PLEASURES OF ENGLAND. The Oxford Lectures of 1883 and 1884.
[*14th Thousand*

LOVE'S MEINIE. On Greek and English Birds. [*9th Thousand*

Cloth Boxes to hold Six Volumes, 1s. each.

Ruskin Treasuries

A Series of Little Books on

LIFE, ART, LITERATURE, ECONOMY,
etc., etc.

Demy 32mo, cloth, 6d. *net* each }
Leather gilt, 1s. *net* each } Ruskin's Motto on Cover.

Calf gilt, cover design, yapp edge, 1s. 6d. *net.*

Cloth Boxes to hold the Set, 8d. each.

WEALTH.	EDUCATION AND YOUTH.
ECONOMY.	THE DIGNITY OF MAN.
WOMEN AND DRESS.	ART.
GIRLHOOD.	ARCHITECTURE.
LIBERTY AND GOVERNMENT.	RELIGION.
OF VULGARITY.	MAXIMS.

Dictionaries and Reference Books

ENGLISH QUOTATIONS. By Col. P. H. DALBIAC. Demy 8vo, cloth. 7s. 6d.
Cheap Edition, 3s. 6d. net. [Fifth Edition.
CLASSICAL QUOTATIONS. By T. B. HARBOTTLE. Demy 8vo, cloth, 7s. 6d.
[Second Edition.
CONTINENTAL QUOTATIONS (FRENCH AND ITALIAN). By Col. P. H. DALBIAC
and T. B. HARBOTTLE. Demy 8vo, cloth. 7s. 6d.
FRENCH QUOTATIONS. Crown 8vo, cloth. 3s. 6d. net.
ITALIAN QUOTATIONS. Crown 8vo, cloth. 3s. 6d. net.
GERMAN QUOTATIONS. By L. DALBIAC. Demy 8vo. 7s. 6d.
Cheap Edition, crown 8vo, 3s. 6d. net.
SPANISH QUOTATIONS. By Major M. HUME and T. B. HARBOTTLE.
Demy 8vo, cloth. 7s. 6d.
LATIN QUOTATIONS. By T. B. HARBOTTLE. Crown 8vo, cloth. 3s. 6d. net.
ORIENTAL QUOTATIONS (ARABIC AND PERSIAN). By CLAUD FIELD.
Large crown 8vo. 7s. 6d.
DICTIONARY OF CONTEMPORARY QUOTATIONS (ENGLISH). With
Authors and Subjects Indexes. By HELENA SWAN.
Small Demy 8vo, cloth, 7s. 6d. Crown 8vo Edition. 3s. 6d. net.
WHAT GREAT MEN HAVE SAID ABOUT GREAT MEN: A DICTIONARY OF
QUOTATIONS. By WILLIAM WALE. Demy 8vo, cloth. 7s. 6d.

DICTIONARY OF HISTORICAL ALLUSIONS. By T. B. HARBOTTLE.
Demy 8vo, cloth, 7s. 6d. Crown 8vo, cloth. 3s. 6d. net.
DICTIONARY OF BATTLES. By T. B. HARBOTTLE. Demy 8vo, cloth, 7s. 6d.
Cheap Edition, crown 8vo. 3s. 6d. net.
DICTIONARY OF POLITICAL PHRASES AND ALLUSIONS. By HUGH
MONTGOMERY and PHILIP G. CAMBRAY. Small Demy 8vo. 7s. 6d
A DICTIONARY OF ABBREVIATIONS. By W. T. ROGERS.
Crown 8vo, cloth. 7s. 6d.
DICTIONARY OF LEGAL ABBREVIATIONS. By W. T. ROGERS.
Large Crown 8vo, cloth. 2s. 6d.

DICTIONARY OF INDIAN BIOGRAPHY. Short Biographical Notices of more
than 2,000 persons connected with India (European and Native)·from A.D. 1750
downwards. By C. E. BUCKLAND, C.I.E. Small Demy 8vo, cloth, 7s. 6d.
Cheap Edition, crown 8vo, 3s. 6d. net.
FAMOUS SAYINGS AND THEIR AUTHORS: A COLLECTION OF HISTORICAL
SAYINGS IN ENGLISH, FRENCH, GERMAN, GREEK, ITALIAN, AND LATIN.
With Authors and Subjects Indexes. By E. LATHAM. Second Edition.
Small Demy 8vo, cloth, 7s. 6d. Colonial Edition, 3s. 6d.
THE BROWNING CYCLOPÆDIA. A Guide to the Study of the Works of
Robert Browning. With Copious Explanatory Notes and References on all
difficult passages. By EDWARD BERDOE, Revised. Sixth Edition.
Small 8vo, cloth, 10s. 6d. Colonial Edition, cloth, 3s. 6d.

Books by Henry Grey, F.Z.S.

All Crown 8vo, Cloth.

A KEY TO THE WAVERLEY NOVELS. Eighth Thousand. 2s. 6d.
A POCKET ENCYCLOPÆDIA OF USEFUL KNOWLEDGE. 1s.
[Third Thousand.
A BIRD'S-EYE VIEW OF ENGLISH LITERATURE. Sixth Thousand. 1s.
TROWEL, CHISEL, AND BRUSH. A Concise Manual of Architecture, Sculpture,
and Painting. Fourth Thousand. 1s.
THE CLASSICS FOR THE MILLION. Nineteenth Thousand. 3s. 6d.
PLOTS OF SOME OF THE MOST FAMOUS OLD ENGLISH PLAYS. 2s. 6d.